THE
RANGERS
MISCELLANY

THE
RANGERS
MISCELLANY

BY ROBERT McELROY

Vision Sports Publishing
19–23 High Street,
Kingston upon Thames
Surrey KT1 1LL

www.visionsp.co.uk

Published by Vision Sports Publishing 2009

Text © Robert McElroy
Illustrations © Bob Bond Sporting Caricatures

ISBN 13: 978-1-905326-72-3

Printed and bound in UK by
MPG Books, Bodmin

Typeset by Palimpsest Book Production Limited,
Grangemouth, Stirlingshire

A CIP catalogue record for this book is
available from the British Library

Mixed Sources
Product group from well-managed
forests and other controlled sources
www.fsc.org Cert no. SA-COC-1565
© 1996 Forest Stewardship Council

FSC

Vision Sports Publishing are
proud that this book is made
from paper certified by the
Forest Stewardship Council

Foreword
by John Greig

When, as a 16 year-old youth from Edinburgh, I signed for Rangers Football Club, it was a decision that would change my life forever. The sheer vastness of the club and of the old stadium made an immediate impression; the imposing figure of Manager Scot Symon welcomed me in his oak-panelled office at the top of the marble staircase and my first full-time wage was the grand sum of £10 a week!

I learned at an early age that success was expected. I was very fortunate to make my first-team debut in one of the greatest teams in the club's history; that of the early '60's that included players of the class of Jim Baxter and Ian McMillan, Jimmy Millar, Ralph Brand and Davie Wilson. I made my debut in one of the old-style League Cup sectional ties in September 1961 against Airdrieonians at Ibrox, and was lucky enough to score in a 4–1 win, but it was a close-season tour of the Soviet Union the following summer that presented me with my major breakthrough. National Service prevented the legendary Jim Baxter from travelling, and with his natural understudy Billy Stevenson having walked out on the club, the opportunity presented itself for me to step into the breach – even though at that time I was regarded as an inside-forward.

It meant a great deal to me to follow in the footsteps of the great players who had featured in the club's history. It was an even greater honour to be named captain in 1965 – David Meiklejohn, Jock Shaw and George Young were amongst the great names who had trodden that path before me.

I can recall as a youngster travelling through from Edinburgh by train in the company of Jimmy Millar, Ralph Brand, and Billy Stevenson. It was an education in itself, learning from a trio of experienced players.

In all I played 755 competitive games for Rangers, scoring no fewer than 120 goals – not bad for a defender or midfield player. The first trophy was a milestone in my career; the League Championship triumph of 1962/63, which was quickly followed by the Scottish Cup that same season in the first 'Old Firm' final for an incredible 35 years. So many successes followed. In all my career at Ibrox produced five League titles, six Scottish Cups and four League Cups. Three Trebles were the pinnacle – in 1964, 1976 and 1978 – not forgetting the 1973 Centenary Scottish Cup Final when, following our 3–2 win over Celtic, it was a great honour to be presented with the trophy by HRH The Princess Alexandra.

The highlight of course was the 1972 European Cup Winners Cup triumph in Barcelona. It was the third time the club had reached a European final and defeat was not an option. Five years earlier we had reached the final of the same tournament but, against Bayern Munich, we were handicapped by the game being staged in Nuremberg. I felt for our fans in Barcelona, however, to be denied the chance to see us lifting the trophy was cruel. The whole event was badly organised by our Spanish hosts. There were lean spells too of course, but perhaps such periods make one stronger.

I was also honoured to represent Scotland 44 times, captaining my country for fully four years. This included the historic 1967 win at Wembley over World Cup holders England; the second triumph over the 'Auld Enemy' of my career for on my international debut at Hampden Park in 1964 an Alan Gilzean header had secured a 1–0 home victory. Few goals have been screened as often as my last-minute winner against Italy at Hampden on 9th November 1965 in a World Cup qualifier. In the return tie in Naples I led my country for the first time, although our team was ravaged by injuries, going down 0–3 and thus being denied the opportunity to play in the 1966 World Cup Finals in England.

I played for, and captained, Rangers under four managers – Scot Symon, David White, Willie Waddell and Jock Wallace – and learned a great deal from all of them. But I had never imagined that one day I would sit in the Manager's Office in my own right.

I was awarded a Testimonial Match by the club in 1978; the first Rangers player to be so honoured since Davie Meiklejohn half-a-century earlier. It was to prove to be the last time that the old ground was filled to capacity for the following season redevelopment work commenced on the new stadium. Equally, to be voted as the 'Greatest Ever Ranger' by the Ibrox fans themselves meant so much to me.

There have been days of great sadness too. The Ibrox Disaster of 1971 cost the lives of 66 Rangers fans who simply left home to attend a football match. There is never a day that passes without my thoughts going back to that tragic day. The stadium of today, one of Europe's finest, is a fitting memorial to their memory.

This is more than just a football club; it is an institution that means so much to so many people worldwide. Even today, more than half-a-century after I first gazed on the imposing facade that is the Main Stand at Ibrox Stadium, it still gives me a special thrill every time I turn into Edmiston Drive.

John Greig, MBE

Acknowledgements

My thanks to Jim Drewett, Toby Trotman and all the staff at Vision Sports Publishing for their help and assistance in the production of this book.

Special thanks to Rangers Legend John Greig, MBE, for the foreword, and finally to my wife Margaret for her continuing help, support and patience.

— HUMBLE ORIGINS —

Now one of the biggest names in world football, Rangers Football Club grew out of the most humble of origins. Formed by four young students in 1872, the club's fledgling days were spent on the public pitches of Glasgow Green.

When brothers Peter and Moses McNeil, Peter Campbell and William McBeath took a leisurely walk in the West End Park (a Glasgow open space long gone, in the present area of Kelvinbridge), they decided to form their own football club, having been intrigued by the growing popularity of the game.

These four young men hailed from villages along the Gare Loch, from Rhu to Garelochhead, some 30 miles from Glasgow. All four were still in their teens, with Moses the youngest at just 16.

Friends and student colleagues were recruited, and the club was christened The Rangers, from the name of an English rugby club that Moses had noted. A second-hand ball was purchased and training commenced – on every evening save the Sabbath.

Rangers were to all intents and purposes a boys' club – and after several weeks of concentrated training a challenge match was arranged towards the end of May 1872 against Callendar FC. A goalless draw ensued in what was a hard-fought game.

That opening match had been played in the Flesher's Haugh area of Glasgow Green, on the public pitches. Soon after the game the club held a formal meeting and elected office bearers, with Peter McNeil being given the responsibility of claiming the desired pitch for future matches by arriving early on Saturday mornings. For the club's second game (against a team called Clyde – not the current club), the players wore light blue jerseys for the first time.

For these early matches in the club's history the players would change into their playing kits behind a clump of trees, paying a young boy to stand guard over their everyday clothes during the game. The whole Rangers set-up at this time could scarcely have been more basic.

— CLUB COLOURS —

Rangers' colours have almost always been light blue – but the shade of blue was in fact originally of a much lighter hue than today. Until the 1930s the Rangers blue was similar to that of Manchester City, Olympique Marseille or Napoli today, before the change to a royal blue colour that endures to this day. In 1882 in an effort to provide a catalyst for a change of fortune on the field of play, a change to a hooped blue-and-white strip was introduced, but after less than a year the club reverted to their traditional light blue.

— A FIRST SCOTTISH CUP FINAL —

In time the young Rangers had established one particular pitch on Glasgow Green as their own. Then, three years later, the club acquired a ground of their own at Burnbank in the West End of the city, not far from the West End Park that had given birth to the club. In 1876 Great Western Road was vacated as the club moved south of the river for the first time – to Kinning Park. During their first season at 'KP' the young students remarkably reached the Scottish FA Cup Final for the first time. Their opponents were the Vale of Leven, from Alexandria, one of the giants of the game at the time.

That 1877 Scottish Cup Final saw Rangers very much the underdogs against older, more experienced and physically stronger opponents – yet the final would go to three games before the Vale emerged victorious 3–2. The sequence of three ties brought the young Rangers to the public attention and they became increasingly popular.

There would be difficult times ahead – but a Scottish institution had been born. Over the coming years, the growth and development of Rangers Football Club from its humble origins in the 1870s to a multi-million pound business with millions of fans worldwide would represent one of the great romantic stories in sporting history.

— EURO BLUES —

Some fan stories from Rangers' numerous European adventures:

- Thousands of Light Blue followers invaded London for the Cup Winners' Cup first leg with Tottenham Hotspur in 1962, the thoroughfares around White Hart Lane being swamped by a blue tide. One cockney ticket tout found to his cost that Scottish football fans don't appreciate being held to ransom for the much sought-after briefs. While he stood proudly displaying perhaps a dozen tickets pinned to his coat, a Rangers supporters' bus pulled up beside him and within seconds he was denuded of both coat and tickets as the bus drove off.

- An away victory in Europe was something of a rarity back in the mid-1980s (sadly, it still is today) but following the UEFA Cup win over Boavista in 1986 a group of Rangers fans celebrated in the Hotel Meridian (just around the corner from the ground). As the champagne flowed freely, one member of the group posed an optimistic question: "If we go all the way in the UEFA Cup this season and win the tournament, whilst at the same time winning the league, then next season triumph in the European Cup – will we be the first team ever to annex all three European trophies?"

  The answer was no – Juventus had already done so, but at this early stage of the Souness Revolution, and just six months after Rangers had scraped into Europe courtesy of fifth place in the Scottish league, it was reassuring to know that Rangers' fans were keeping their feet on the ground.

- On a trip to Bucharest in the European Cup in 1988 one visiting fan sat watching the entire match against Steau in a sleeveless Rangers top, despite the sub-zero temperatures. An enquiry on his well-being from a fellow fan met with the response: "I'm absolutely freezing, mate. Don't understand it at all – it was a lovely morning when I left Glasgow . . ."

- It was bitterly cold in Dortmund when the Light Blue legions visited the city for a UEFA Cup tie in December 1999. On the afternoon of the game the city authorities laid on a welcome for both sets of fans in Dortmund's main square. Amongst the souvenir stalls were two dispensing free beer and free soup – and, almost unbelievably, there was a bigger queue for the soup!

- When Rangers were drawn against Ilves Tampere in 1986 one fan flew in to Helsinki from London, where he worked during the week. Upon arrival, flushed with the excitement of travel and under the influence of more than a few drinks from the in-flight bar, he rushed off to telephone his wife, back at the family home in Edinburgh. Unfortunately, he completely forgot that his wife knew nothing of his planned trip, believing him to be working in London all that week!

— SHIRT SPONSORS —

Just four companies have sponsored Rangers' shirts:

1984–87	CR Smith
1987–99	McEwan's Lager
1999–2003	NTL
2003–present	Carling

— TOP HITMEN —

Rangers' goalscoring records:

All games	Ally McCoist (1983–98) 432
Competitive fixtures	Jimmy Smith (1928–46) 382
League games	Jimmy Smith (1928–46) 299
	(includes 74 wartime)
	Ally McCoist (1983–98) 251
European games	Ally McCoist (1983–98) 21

— RANGERS LEGENDS: TOM VALLANCE (1873–84) —

Tom Valance: Long jumper, painter and Rangers legend

Tom Vallance was one of the club's earliest pioneers. Not quite a founding member when the Rangers Football Club was formed in February 1872, he became a member in the spring of 1873.

Born in 1856 on a farm at Succoth, near Renton, Dunbarton-shire, Tom Vallance instantly felt at home amongst the young lads from the Gare Loch who had given birth to what would in time become a Scottish institution.

Vallance captained Rangers for nine years in the struggling early days when Rangers were just one of many young teams.

He led the club to its very first trophy success – the Glasgow Merchants' Charity Cup of 1879, when Vale of Leven were defeated 2–1 at the First Hampden Park before 11,000 spectators.

He captained the team on three home grounds (Fleshers' Haugh, Burnbank and Kinning Park), and led the Light Blues in their first two Scottish Cup Finals – again against Vale of Leven in 1877 and 1879.

An athlete as well as a footballer, he was principally a full back. He boasted a tall, slim physique but nevertheless was strong in the tackle despite his willowy frame. The lack of newspaper coverage of Scottish football in the early years makes it impossible to say with precision how many times he played for the club, but it was likely that he made many more than the 146 appearances that are recorded.

A club man to his core, he would sometimes help collect gate money shortly before kick-off, as one contemporary account records: "On special match days I have seen the tall, swanky figure of handsome Tom Vallance, garbed ready for the fray on the field of battle, gathering in the shekels as George Cameron, Jake Hamilton and others who helped with the rolling of the turf and the rude appliances for the bathing of the players, held the human stream at bay."

One of the club's first internationals, Vallance played a remarkable seven times for Scotland at a time when there were no more than two games per year. He was the first Rangers player to be selected for the prestigious encounter with England and enjoyed three wins in his four appearances against the Auld Enemy. Of these victories, two were by record scores – 7–2 at First Hampden in 1878 and 6–1 at Kennington Oval three years later.

Vallance was also something of a Scottish Renaissance man or 'lad o' pairts'. He was a noted oarsman, held the Scottish long-jump record for 14 years from 1881 with a leap of almost 22 feet, and had paintings exhibited by the Royal Scottish Academy.

When his playing career came to an end due to ill health, Vallance served Rangers as president from 1883 to 1889. During his term of office the club moved from Kinning Park to First

Ibrox, the decision proving to be a key one in its long-term growth.

One of the real Corinthian spirits in the early Victorian period, Vallance may not have amassed the medal tally of future club captains but without men of his calibre in those initial years there would be no Rangers Football Club today.

Tom Vallance factfile
Born: Succoth, Dunbartonshire 27th May 1856
Died: 16th February 1935
Appearances: 146
Full international appearances while at Rangers: 7 caps for Scotland
Honours:
Glasgow Merchants' Charity Cup: 1879
Scottish FA Cup (finalist): 1877, 1879

— RIGHT ROYAL OCCASIONS —

There have been numerous links between Rangers Football Club and the Royal Family:

- In 1902 the final of the British League Cup, a tournament organised to raise funds following the Ibrox Disaster of 5th April, saw Rangers face Celtic at First Cathkin. The match, which Celtic won 3–2 after extra time, was delayed until 17th June in order that it would coincide with the Coronation of King Edward VII.
- His Majesty King George VI and Queen Elizabeth visited Ibrox on Tuesday 3rd May 1938 to open the Empire Exhibition. 100,000 spectators were present to see the ceremony, and later that evening 6,000 returned to see Rangers defeat Clyde 4–1 in the Glasgow Merchants' Charity Cup.
- The King had been following in the footsteps of his father, George V, who had held an investiture at Ibrox on 18th

September 1917 in the dark days of the Great War. An enormous crowd assembled to watch His Majesty present medals and decorations to a number of officers, non-commissioned officers, and other servicemen, and to the next of kin of those who had fallen in battle. At the conclusion of proceedings, Rangers' chairman Sir John Ure Primrose and manager/secretary William Wilton were presented to the King by Glasgow's Lord Provost, Thomas Dunlop. The King expressed his delight with all the arrangements. The proceedings at Ibrox bore the official hallmark, and both Rangers Football Club and Ibrox Stadium had the distinction of their names being recorded in the Court Circular, a framed copy of which (chronicling the day's proceedings) hung in the Ibrox Pavilion thereafter.

- Accompanied by her husband Lord Snowdon, Princess Margaret visited Ibrox in August 1962, meeting chairman John Lawrence, manager Scot Symon, and other officials.
- On the occasion of the centenary Scottish Cup Final in 1973 at Hampden Park, Her Royal Highness the Princess Alexandra presented the trophy to Rangers captain John Greig following a 3–2 win over Celtic.
- The most recent member of the Royal Family to visit Ibrox Stadium was Her Royal Highness the Princess Royal on 20th May 2000, attending a meeting of one of her charities in a function suite.

— HANDY WITH BAT AND BALL —

Two Rangers players have been capped for Scotland at both football and cricket. Scot Symon played against Hungary at Ibrox in 1938, and was a fine cricketer for Perthshire for many years. He holds the distinction of being the first man to be capped by Scotland at both sports. Andy Goram also achieved this feat, being capped 43 times at football, whilst in 1989 he played twice for Scotland against Ireland and Australia (the latter at Hamilton Crescent, scene of Rangers' very first Scottish FA Cup Final appearance).

— RANGERS LEGENDS: JOHN MCPHERSON
(1890–1902) —

John McPherson: Versatile player who became a club director

John McPherson was described at the club's Jubilee Dinner in the 1922/23 season as the finest player in the then 50-year history of the club. It was a not unworthy accolade. He was perhaps the most versatile player ever to wear the Light Blue, appearing in every position, including goal, during his 12 years in Govan.

An engine fitter by trade, McPherson mainly played as an inside forward. He was a marvellous dribbler, but was also blessed with a goalscorer's natural instinct and great strength. A superb tactician, in many respects it was he who welded the many individual stars of the 1890s Rangers into a team.

'Kitey' was already a full Scotland international when he signed for Rangers on 25th June 1890, having previously played for his native Kilmarnock and Cowlairs, a senior Springburn club of the time. He scored seven goals in nine games for his country, including a last-minute winner at Kennington Oval against England in 1889 as the Scots won 3–2. One year later McPherson scored Scotland's goal in a 1–1 draw with the Auld Enemy at Second Hampden (later renamed Second Cathkin Park).

His goalscoring ratio at club level was an impressive 176 goals in 327 games, including 15 in 18 in his first season at First Ibrox, 1890/91 (the inaugural season of Scottish league football). He scored in Rangers' very first league game – a 5–2 home win over Hearts, then followed that up with nine goals in the next three.

He hit five goals in a match on two occasions, in an 8–2 defeat of St Mirren at First Ibrox in 1890 and a 9–2 mauling away to Abercorn (a defunct Paisley club) six years later.

McPherson scored in both the 1894 and 1897 Scottish Cup Finals, the first Rangers player to net in two. He also scored in four Glasgow Cup Finals and the 1897 Charity Cup – all of which were won by Rangers.

In his final season with the club, 1901/02, he played the full 90 minutes in goal in a crucial home league fixture against St Mirren – Rangers won 3–2. Nor was this his first appearance in the position for the Ibrox men. One year earlier, over Easter, Rangers played two games in two days in Belfast against Linfield. In the first at the Cliftonville Grounds, Kitey scored twice as the Glasgow club triumphed 8–1. 24 hours later at the Balmoral Grounds, it was a more modest 4–2 win for the visitors with McPherson between the posts.

McPherson, whose brother David also played for Rangers between 1891 and 1893, retired in 1902. He was appointed a club director five years later – a post he held until his death in 1926 whilst watching the Clyde Sports at Shawfield.

John McPherson factfile
Born: Kilmarnock, 19th June 1868
Died: 31st July 1926
Appearances: 327
Goals: 176
Full international appearances while at Rangers: 5 caps for Scotland
Honours:
League championship: 1890/91, 1898/99, 1899/1900, 1900/01
Scottish FA Cup: 1894, 1897, 1898
Glasgow League: 1896, 1898
Glasgow Cup: 1892/93, 1893/94, 1896/97, 1897/98, 1899/1900, 1900/01
Glasgow Merchants' Charity Cup: 1897, 1900

— HISTORY OF THE GROUNDS: EARLY YEARS —

"A playing field becomes like a friend, and the wrench
at parting is a bit stiff." *Scottish Umpire* (1899)

No one alive today has known any other home to Rangers than Ibrox Stadium, but in actual fact the ground is the fifth that the club has called home.

The first, when the club was founded in 1872, could not have been more humble or basic – the public pitches of the Fleshers' Haugh on Glasgow Green where Rangers played their home games for three years until 1875. Conditions were spartan and basic and a team member had to arrive early on a Saturday morning to secure the use of the desired pitch, although in time it was accepted that one pitch in particular was for the use of the Rangers. The 'dressing rooms' were in fact a shrubbery where the players changed into their playing kit, a small boy being employed to look after the everyday clothes.

A home of their own was secured in 1875 when the club moved to Burnbank, off Great Western Road in the West End of the city, near Kelvinbridge and the West End Park which had given birth to the club. They stayed for just one season before moving over to the south side of the city, never to leave it, into Clydesdale's former home at Kinning Park. The 'Dale were moving to Titwood, where they remain to this day albeit only as a cricket club.

Kinning Park was good for Rangers. Its proximity to the shipyards meant that the club's home games attracted a large following as the workers downed tools of a Saturday lunchtime before heading to the football, possibly via a local hostelry. The ground lay just off West Scotland Street. Vale of Leven provided the opposition for Rangers' first game at their new home (as indeed they had at Burnbank), attracting 1,500 spectators. The capacity of the ground grew from 2,000 to 7,000 during Rangers' 11-year tenure as regular improvements were made with the addition of sloping terraces. 'KP' was a real home to Rangers, and it was with regret that they were obliged to move in 1887 when the landlord gave notice of the termination of the lease due to a planned industrial development. It is a historical quirk in the club's history that the final official match at Kinning Park was an FA Cup quarter-final tie against Old Westminsters, won 5–1. This was the 'Gers' only FA Cup campaign, and that victory sent them into the semi-finals where they went down 3–1 to Aston Villa at Crewe. The Scottish Football Association subsequently banned its member clubs from participating in the competition.

— SCOT-LESS IN ATHENS —

When Rangers drew 1–1 with Panathinaikos in Athens in a Champions League fixture on 1st October 2003 the Light Blue line-up, including substitutes, consisted entirely of non-Scots for the first time in the club's history:

Stefan Klos (Germany)
Zurab Khizanishvili (Georgia)
Craig Moore (Australia)
Henning Berg (Norway)
Michael Ball (England)

Nuno Capucho (Portugal)
Mikel Arteta (Spain)
Emerson (Brazil)
Peter Løvenkrands (Denmark)
Michael Mols (Netherlands)
Shota Arveladze (Georgia)
Subs: Paolo Vanoli (Italy)
Christian Nerlinger (Germany)

— CELEBRITY FANS —

Arnold Palmer
Legendary golfer whose presence at the Centenary Open at St Andrews in 1960 resurrected the championship. Palmer won seven majors between 1958 and 1964 – the Open Championships of 1961 and 1962, the US Masters of 1958, 1960, 1962 and 1964, and the 1960 US Open. Also a shareholder of the club.

Gary Player
Top-class South Africa-born golfer who won the Open Championships of 1959, 1968 and 1974, the US Masters of 1961 and 1974, and the 1965 US Open.

Sean Connery
Originally a Celtic fan, he saw the light and defected to Rangers in the early 1990s, principally through his friendship with chairman David Murray. A regular attendee at Ibrox, he has frequently travelled abroad to watch the Light Blues. Connery's acting career has been both successful and one of considerable durability, his most famous role being perhaps that of British agent James Bond.

Andrew Neil
Former editor of *The Scotsman* who is now a television presenter on such programmes as *This Week* and *The Daily Politics*.

Gordon Ramsay
Celebrity chef and television personality. Awarded two Michelin

stars for his creative reputation as an outstanding chef, his television career has gone from strength to strength with such shows as *Ramsay's Kitchen Nightmares* and *The F Word*. As a youth he had a spell with Rangers in the mid-1980s, but has tried to embellish his Ibrox career with stories of how he played two first-team games and was all set for an extended run until injury ended his career. Not true – his solitary appearance beyond the youth team was in a testimonial game at East Kilbride when Rangers fielded what was very much a reserve team.

Alistair Burnett
Journalist and news-reader who was for many years the main presenter on ITN's flagship news programme *News at Ten*.

Robert Carlyle
Actor, who has appeared in films such as *Trainspotting*, *The Full Monty* and *The World Is Not Enough*.

Midge Ure
One-time lead singer with Ultravox and Band Aid organiser:

Carol Smillie
Television presenter.

Graeme Dott
2006 World Snooker Champion. He subsequently paraded the trophy at Ibrox during the interval of a 2–0 league win over Hearts, having received permission from the sponsors 888.com to adorn the silverware with blue ribbons. The sponsor's traditional colour was green!

Andy Fordham
World Darts Champion nicknamed 'the Viking'.

Alan McGee
Founder of the record company Creation Records, McGee also discovered the band Oasis.

Nick Nairn
Another celebrity chef and television personality.

Colin Montgomerie
Scots golfer, winner of European Order of Merit on numerous occasions and a key member of the Great Britain and Europe Ryder Cup team for many years. 'Monty' has just missed out on a major on numerous occasions and, now in the twilight of his career, appears unlikely to ever break his duck. Appointed 2010 Ryder Cup Captain.

Kirsty Young
Television newsreader.

John Smeaton
Baggage handler who sprang to the help of police during the Glasgow Airport terrorist attack in July 2007. Later that month he was presented on the Ibrox pitch before the pre-season fixture with Chelsea.

— THE 1902 IBROX DISASTER —

As the 1900s dawned there was no doubt that Rangers had established themselves at the very forefront of Scottish football, with a magnificent new ground and as league champions for four consecutive seasons from 1898/99 to 1901/02.

There was fierce competition among the three Glasgow footballing giants of the day, however, to build the biggest and best ground in order to secure the award of the major games – the Scottish Cup Final and the biannual Scotland–England fixture. In 1900 Celtic Park had hosted the latter, but Ibrox won the right to stage the 1901 final and both show games in 1902, by which time the arena had been extended to accommodate some 80,000 spectators, although the record attendance pre-April 1902 stood at a 'mere' 40,000.

The Scotland-England international of 5th April 1902 was to be the crowning glory for Rangers' magnificent home. Weather conditions on the morning of the game were much more favourable than those earlier in the week. Heavy rain was falling, however, as the game kicked off before an enthusiastic near-capacity crowd of 68,114, which smashed all previous records. The gates remained open as still more people surged in, causing those already within the enclosure to seek a better and more comfortable vantage point. Hundreds poured from the eastern terrace along the side of the pitch towards the western end of the ground, climbing the long narrow stairways to the very top of that terracing. As the rain poured down relentlessly, the crowd began to sway as they followed the flow of the game, and people at the foot of the terrace spilled onto the grass behind the goal.

At the very top of that heaving sea of humanity many felt the ground trembling under their feet as rows of steel uprights which held the wooden planks upon which spectators stood began to groan. With a sickening crack, the terracing gave way as seven rows of planking disappeared and with them hundreds of spectators swallowed up in a hole some 50 feet long and 12 feet wide, dropping 40 feet to the ground below.

One eyewitness described the scene as the terracing simply "collapsing like a trapdoor," a huge gap appearing without warning, without noise. 26 people were to die, some 587 more were injured, and yet incredibly the game was allowed to continue after an 18-minute hold-up, caused by fans spilling on to the field of play as spectators moved away from the scene of the disaster. Unbelievably, the broken terrace was quickly reoccupied once the game had restarted, in spite of the obvious risks or the gory scenes below. Most of the crowd were barely aware of what had happened, which led one newspaper to observe, "Nothing could better illustrate the vastness of this stadium than that 400 people should drop through a hole and the rest remain in ignorance."

The decision to restart the game was widely condemned. "Not even the cries of dying sufferers nor the sight of broken limbs could attract this football maddened crowd from gazing upon their beloved sport," wrote one correspondent. Officials later defended their decision by explaining that they feared a greater disaster had the game been abandoned. As play raged on rescue workers treated the injured and dying whilst listening to the cheering crowd. Broken wood was used as stretchers and splints while the corridors of the stands became emergency first-aid stations.

Sympathy and offers of support flooded into Rangers from all over the country, with games being arranged by many clubs to raise money for the Ibrox Disaster Benefit Fund. The disaster was chilling proof that more solid methods of stadium construction would be required in future. No longer would the simplistic design of wooden terraces built on an iron framework be considered safe to house the enormous attendances that in the early days of the 20th century were being attracted to football grounds. Henceforth, stadia would be built on foundations of solid earth and later concrete, whilst retaining the oval bowl shape that had become so popular in offering the best viewing of the field of play.

The disaster had a serious long-term effect on Rangers' dominant position in Scottish football. A total of 22 players were immediately made available for transfer both for the benefit of the Disaster Fund and in order to pay for the reconstruction work now so essential. A period of transition followed, and it would be nine more years before Rangers reclaimed the league championship.

— MILESTONE LEAGUE GOALSCORERS —

Date	Goal no.	Scorer	Result
16th Aug 1890	1	Jimmy Adams (og)	Rangers 5 Hearts 2
8th Dec 1906	1,000	Alec Smith	Clyde 1 Rangers 5
15th Sept 1919	2,000	Jimmy Gordon	Kilmarnock 1 Rangers 7
20th Dec 1930	3,000	Bob McGowan	Rangers 7 Cowdenbeath 0
25th Dec 1947	4,000	Jimmy Duncanson	Dundee 1 Rangers 3
29th April 1961	5,000	Alex Scott	Rangers 7 Ayr United 3
19th Jan 1974	6,000	Derek Parlane	Hearts 2 Rangers 4
9th Dec 1989	7,000	Ally McCoist	Rangers 3 Motherwell 1
10th Aug 2002	8,000	Shota Arveladze	Rangers 3 Dundee 0

— RANGERS LEGENDS: ALEC SMITH (1894–1915) —

Alec Smith: Scorer of Rangers' 1000th league goal

An Ayrshire lad, Alec Smith arrived at First Ibrox from the Darvel lace mills in April 1894 as a 17-year-old. He did not depart until the dark days of the Great War, serving the club for fully 21 years – a length of service beaten only by Dougie Gray in the club's history.

An outside left who preceded Alan Morton with both Rangers and Scotland, Smith might be rated as the most outstanding player ever produced in the position in Scottish football apart from 'the Wee Society Man' himself. Unlike most wingers, he was a player of great consistency. He was also remarkably energetic, full of running and constantly seeking the ball. In short, he was the complete winger – a dribbler supreme possessing pace, ball control and a trademark swerving knee-high cross which he could produce from all angles on the run.

Smith was a key member of the first great Rangers side which won four consecutive league titles between 1898 and 1902. The sequence would surely have been extended but for the requirement to raise funds following the 1902 Ibrox Disaster. He played in every game of the famous 1898/99 league championship campaign when Rangers achieved an incredible 100 per cent record, a feat unmatched in world football. In all, he won seven league titles and three Scottish Cups and was also a member of the side that won the 1901/02 Glasgow International Exhibition Cup. In December 1906, in a 5–1 win over Clyde at Shawfield, Smith also had the distinction of scoring Rangers' 1,000th league goal.

He played 21 times in the Dark Blue, including the 1902 Ibrox Disaster clash with England that was later decreed unofficial. Remarkably, he made 12 consecutive appearances for Scotland at a time when no more than three internationals were played per season. In 1900, he featured in the historic 4–1 drubbing of England when the home side wore the primrose and pink racing colours of Lord Rosebery, and the following year he played in the Scotland side that demolished Ireland 11–0 – a record score that stands to this day.

In his memoirs, published shortly before his death in 1954, Smith recalled the Rangers brake clubs' (the Victorian equivalent of today's supporters' clubs) convoy up Glasgow's Buchanan Street following trophy successes – the blue flags fluttering in the breeze. Sadly, such a parade would be out of the question today – if for no other reason than that Buchanan Street is now pedestrianised!

Alec Smith factfile
Born: Darvel, Ayrshire, 7th November 1876
Died: 12th November 1954

Appearances: 653
Goals: 201
Full international appearances while at Rangers: 20 caps for
Scotland
Honours:
League championship: 1898/99, 1899/1900, 1900/01, 1901/02,
1910/11, 1911/12, 1912/13
Scottish FA Cup: 1897, 1898, 1903
Glasgow League: 1896, 1898
Glasgow Cup: 1896/97, 1897/98, 1899/1900, 1900/01, 1901/02,
1910/11, 1911/12, 1912/13, 1913/14
Glasgow Merchants' Charity Cup: 1897, 1900, 1904, 1906,
1907, 1909, 1911
Glasgow International Exhibition Cup: 1901/02
Scottish National Exhibition Tournament: 1908/09

— DEADLY IN THE DERBY —

Rangers' top scorers in Old Firm matches are:

1. RC Hamilton (1897–1906)	36 (includes seven non-competitive)
2. Ally McCoist (1983–98)	27
3. Jimmy Duncanson (1939–51)	22
4. John McPherson (1890–1902)	20 (includes three non-competitive)
5. Alex Venters (1933–46)	18

— BIG OCCASION PLAYER —

When Rangers defeated Morton 1–0 in the 1948 Scottish FA Cup
Final replay the only goal of the game, scored deep into extra
time, came from a diving header by Billy Williamson, playing in
his first Scottish Cup tie for the club. In the following year's
campaign, 'Sailor' Williamson did not feature in any Scottish
Cup match until being selected for the final against Clyde, scoring
in the Light Blues' 4–1 win. Two games, two goals, two winners'
medals – not a bad record!

— RANGERS MANAGERS: WILLIAM WILTON
(1899–1920) —

William Wilton was Rangers' first manager, and a man who served the club from the time when he signed as a player at the age of just 17 in 1883. It was as an administrator that he would make his real mark, however: first, as honorary match secretary (the equivalent today in some respects of a team manager) for ten years from 1889; then as manager from 1899 until his untimely death in 1920.

Wilton brought great dignity and a keen enthusiasm to the job at a critical time in the club's history, with the introduction of league football and the legalisation of professionalism, not to mention the move from First Ibrox to the site of the present stadium. He was in charge of first-team affairs when Rangers won the inaugural league championship, their first ever Scottish FA Cup, and the world record campaign of 1898/99 when a 100 per cent title record was secured. He also oversaw the recovery following the 1902 Ibrox Disaster, and introduced the Ibrox Sports to the club. A remarkable 38 trophies were won during his 31 years in charge before he tragically drowned at Gourock in 1920.

William Wilton's honours:
League championship: 1890/91,1898/99, 1899/1900, 1900/01, 1901/02, 1910/11, 1911/12, 1912/13, 1917/18, 1919/20
Scottish Cup: 1894, 1897, 1898, 1903
Glasgow Cup: 1892/93, 1893/94, 1896/97, 1897/98, 1899/1900, 1900/01, 1901/02, 1903/04, 1910/11, 1911/12, 1912/13, 1913/14, 1917/18, 1918/19
Glasgow Merchants' Charity Cup: 1897, 1900, 1906, 1907, 1909, 1911, 1919
Glasgow League: 1896, 1898
Glasgow International Exhibition Cup: 1901/02

—GREAT EUROPEAN NIGHTS AT IBROX 1 —

Rangers 2   **Nice 1**
Murray   Faivre
Simpson

1956/57 European Cup, second round, first leg
24th October 1956
Attendance: 65,000

Rangers were the first Scottish champions to qualify for the European Cup – in the inaugural tournament held in the 1955/56 season Hibernian represented Caledonia despite Aberdeen having won the Scottish league in the previous campaign, entry to the first competition being by invitation only.

A first round bye meant that the Light Blues were paired with French champions OGC Nice in the second, with the first leg scheduled for Ibrox. 65,000 spectators produced an electrifying atmosphere on a night of heavy rain and hailstones. The contrast in styles made for an engrossing contest – Rangers the more direct and powerful, playing very much in the traditional British fashion, their opponents exhibiting the Latin style that would provoke so many flashpoints throughout not just this tie but much of the early years of European competition, when the different interpretation of the laws of the game created so much ill-feeling in clashes between British clubs and continental sides.

The French struck first on 23 minutes when Jacques Faivre opened the scoring. Only a superb display of goalkeeping by Dominique Colonna aided by resolute defending from his colleagues and some atrocious finishing kept Nice ahead until shortly before the interval when a Max Murray header levelled the scores.

A second-half siege produced just the one goal through Ulsterman Billy Simpson on the hour – but that 45 minutes was long remembered for two other remarkable incidents, the first when the scores were still tied at 1–1. English referee Arthur Ellis, who had taken charge of the previous year's final in Paris, dramatically called both sets of players together to deliver a lecture, later admitting that his main concern had been the blatant body-checking of the French, then blew for full-time five minutes early – the game having to be restarted after he had realised his error.

Rangers were eventually eliminated after three games by the French champions.

Rangers team: Niven; Shearer, Caldow; McColl, Davis, Logie; Scott, Simpson, Murray, Baird, Hubbard

— THEY SAID IT —

"To be a Ranger is to sense the sacred trust of upholding all that the name means in this shrine of football . . . No true Ranger has ever failed the tradition."
Bill Struth, Rangers manager 1920–54

"Modesty, borne of my close connection with the champions, hampers my eulogising them to the extent that their great performance warrants. A world record, however, especially when it is an unbeatable record, is an achievement that will speak for itself as the years go by."
William Wilton, Rangers honorary match secretary, speaking after the club won every league match in 1898/99

"No man is bigger than the club."   **Bill Struth**

"No comment."
Reticent Rangers manager **Scot Symon**, when telephoned by a sportswriter enquiring about Ibrox weather conditions ahead of a midweek game with much of the city fog-bound

"I was capped for my country, but the greatest honour I ever received was to be appointed captain of Rangers."
Bobby Shearer, Rangers player 1955–65

"If I have one regret in my career, it is that I did not join Rangers a lot sooner."

Ray Wilkins – his previous clubs prior to joining Rangers in 1987 were Chelsea, Manchester United, AC Milan and Paris Saint-Germain

"Can I just say, off the record, no comment . . ."
Ally McCoist, speaking to the press despite a media ban in 1988

"I've told him he's making the biggest mistake of his life."
David Murray on Graeme Souness's departure to Liverpool in April 1991 – Souness later conceded the chairman had been right

"Sorry, Mr Chairman, but you must admit this is the earliest I've been late for some time."
Ally McCoist to Rangers chairman David Murray after missing the start of a Burns Supper

"I only drink when we win a trophy. That's why people think I'm an alcoholic."   **Ian Ferguson**, Rangers player 1988–2000

"We have our bluenoses to go with our orange shirts."
Dick Advocaat, speaking about the 2000 Scottish Cup Final victory over Aberdeen when the Rangers support wore orange Dutch tops in tribute to the Rangers manager

"I'll play professional football for as long as I can, then spend the rest of my life as a manic depressive."
Ally McCoist

"Let the others come after us. We welcome the chase."
Bill Struth

"There's a limit to everyone's patience."
Walter Smith, speaking about Paul Gascoigne in 1996

Gazza!

— NO PASSPORTS REQUIRED —

Rangers have failed to compete in one of the European competitions in just four seasons (1958/59, 1965/66, 1974/75 and 1980/81) since first appearing in the European Cup in 1956.

In 1972/73 Rangers were banned from Europe and denied a chance to defend their Cup Winners' Cup trophy after crowd trouble following their 1972 final victory over Dynamo Moscow in Barcelona. Nevertheless, the Ibrox faithful still had a taste of top-class continental action that season as European Cup holders Ajax took on Rangers in the first ever Super Cup, the Dutch side winning 6–3 on aggregate.

— THE BALLAD OF WILLIE WOODBURN —

Willie Woodburn played for Rangers from 1937 to 1954, winning seven league championship, four Scottish Cup and four League Cup winners' medals. To this day he is regarded by many friends of Rangers as the finest centre half to play for the club since the war. His career ended in controversy when he was suspended *sine die* by the Scottish Football Association after he was sent off four times.

The following words were written in tribute to a Rangers great:

> *His name was Willie Woodburn*
> *And his crime was too much heart*
> *He gave his all for Rangers*
> *On the field of Ibrox Park*
> *And they banished him forever*
> *With a word they call sine die*
> *But the name of Willie Woodburn*
> *In our hearts will never die*
> *Why must he go now?*
> *Why can't he stay?*
> *He gave his all, now he must pay*
> *He played his part each Saturday*
> *And left his heart down Ibrox way*
> *Ask the English down at Wembley*
> *Ask the Welsh, they know his name*
> *Take a trip to dear old Belfast*
> *They'll answer just the same*
> *No matter where you wander*
> *Where they play the football game*
> *There's a legend lives among them*
> *Willie Woodburn is his name*
> *Why must he go now?*
> *Why can't he stay?*
> *He gave it all, now he must pay*
> *He played his part each Saturday*
> *And left his heart down Ibrox way*

— EURO RIVALS —

Rangers have met clubs from the following 34 present-day countries in European competition:

Austria: Graz AK, Rapid Vienna, Sturm Graz
Belgium: Anderlecht, Bruges, Standard Liège
Bulgaria: Levski Sofia, Slavia Sofia
Cyprus: Anorthosis Famagusta
Czech Republic: Dukla Prague, Sparta Prague, Viktoria Žižkov
Denmark: FC Copenhagen, Herfølge, Lyngby
England: Leeds United, Manchester United, Newcastle United, Tottenham Hotspur, Wolverhampton Wanderers
Faroe Islands: Gøtu
Finland: Haka, Ilves
France: Auxerre, Lyon, Marseille, Monaco, Nice, Paris Saint-Germain, St Etienne, Rennes, Strasbourg
Germany: Bayer Leverkusen, Bayern Munich, Borussia Dortmund, Borussia Mönchengladbach, Köln, Dynamo Dresden, Eintracht Frankfurt, Fortuna Düsseldorf, Kaiserslautern, Stuttgart, Werder Bremen, Vorwaerts East Berlin
Greece: AEK Athens, Panathinaikos, PAOK
Hungary: Ferencváros
Israel: Beitar Jerusalem, Hapoel Tel Aviv, Maccabi Haifa
Italy: AC Milan, Fiorentina, Internazionale, Juventus, Livorno, Parma, Torino
Lithuania: FBK Kaunas
Malta: Valetta
Montenegro: Zeta
Netherlands: Ajax, AZ Alkmaar, DWS Amsterdam, Feyenoord, PSV Eindhoven, Sparta Rotterdam, Twente
Northern Ireland: Glentoran
Norway: Lillestrøm, Molde
Poland: Amica Wronki, Górnik Zabrze, Katowice
Portugal: Boavista, Maritimo, Porto, Sporting Lisbon
Republic of Ireland: Bohemians, Dundalk, Shelbourne
Romania: Steau Bucharest
Russia: Alania Vladikavkaz, Anzhi Makhachkala, CSKA Moscow, Dynamo Moscow, Zenit Saint Petersburg

Serbia: FK Vojvodina, Red Star Belgrade, Partizan Belgrade
Slovakia: Artmedia Bratislava, Red Star Bratislava
Slovenia: NK Maribor
Spain: Athletic Bilbao, Barcelona, Osasuna, Real Madrid, Real Zaragoza, Sevilla, Valencia, Villarreal
Sweden: IFK Gothenburg
Switzerland: FC Zürich, Grasshopper-Club Zürich, Young Boys Berne
Turkey: Ankaragücü, Fenerbahçe, Galatasaray
Ukraine: Dynamo Kiev

— RANGERS' TRIPLE CROWNS: 1949 —

Rangers claimed Scotland's first ever Triple Crown – or treble – in the 1948/49 season when they became the first club to win the league championship, Scottish FA Cup and League Cup in the same campaign. Indeed, it had been only since 1946/47 that three national trophy wins had been a possibility with the introduction of the Scottish League Cup following the cessation of hostilities at the end of the Second World War.

Rangers had already secured their place in the history books in 1946/47 when they emerged triumphant from the inaugural League Cup campaign, overwhelming Aberdeen 4–0 in the first final. Two years later it looked likely that the campaign in Scotland's newest tournament would go no further than the group stages when, in a tough section incorporating league champions Hibernian as well as both members of the Old Firm, Rangers secured just two points from their opening three fixtures, trailing Celtic by three points with just three games remaining. However, with the Parkhead men somehow contriving to lose 3–6 at home to Clyde, victory in the remaining three games was enough to send Rangers through to the quarter-finals, including a 2–1 win over Celtic in the final group match watched by 105,000 spectators at Ibrox. Thereafter, wins over St Mirren and Dundee provided the 'Gers with a final appointment with Raith Rovers of Division B, Rangers winning 2–0 courtesy of goals from Torry Gillick and Willie Paton.

The Scottish Cup campaign produced six-figure attendances

at Hampden for Rangers' games in both semi-final and final. East Fife, fourth in the top division that season, were overcome in the last four 3–0 with a Willie Thornton hat-trick, and Clyde vanquished 4–1 in the final.

The league championship race saw the Light Blues unbeaten in the last 12 games, amassing 22 points out of a possible 24. However on the final day Rangers trailed Dundee by one point with both clubs away at Albion Rovers and Falkirk respectively. Astonishingly the Dens men, one win from the title, crashed 1–4 at Brockville – missing a penalty when the game remained goalless – whilst at Cliftonhill Park a Thornton treble in a 4–1 victory made sure the championship trophy would be heading to Glasgow. Rangers thus clinched their first treble in the unlikely setting of Coatbridge.

Leading appearance maker: Bobby Brown, 44 games (ever-present)
Leading goalscorer: Willie Thornton, 34 goals

— OLD FATHER TIME —

The oldest player believed to have played in a first-class game for Rangers was Jock 'Tiger' Shaw who featured in Charlie Johnson's Benefit Match at Palmerston Park, Dumfries at the age of 40 years, 8 months, 26 days. Queen of the South won 3–1 before 8,000 spectators.

In competitive fixtures, Dougie Gray played at the age of 40 years, 7 months, 27 days in a 3–2 home League win against Hibernian before a 25,000 audience on 1st December 1945. Shaw's last competitive outing had come at the age of 39 years, 10 months, 19 days at Bayview Park, Methil, a 20,000 crowd watching East Fife defeat Rangers 3–2 on League business on 18th October 1952.

In more recent times, Walter Smith's second game in charge of a Rangers team – a 1–1 League draw at Pittodrie Park, Aberdeen – saw Peter McCloy in goal aged 39 years, 5 months, 10 days on 26th April 1986 before 17,000 spectators. McCloy's final appearance in Light Blue came three months later in a pre-season friendly at Brockville Park, Falkirk.

David Weir may well yet surpass all of the above . . .

— RANGERS LEGENDS: SANDY ARCHIBALD (1917–34) —

Sandy Archibald: Not bad for £250

A Fifer who had worked in the pits as a miner, Sandy Archibald joined Rangers from Raith Rovers in May 1917 for a transfer fee of just £250. Seldom can any signing have provided better value for money – for the winger went on to play for Rangers for 17 years, appearing in a peacetime record 514 league games for the club.

'The Man from Aberdour' was a solidly built, strong-running player with a powerful shot. For the great majority of his Ibrox career, he formed an electrifying right-wing partnership with Andy Cunningham that created havoc in opposition defences.

On his Rangers debut Archibald played alongside legends of

the ilk of Bert Manderson, James Bowie, Tommy Cairns and Jimmy Gordon. In his final appearance in Light Blue in 1934, he had Tully Craig, Jimmy Smith and Alex Venters for company.

In between, there were many highlights. He scored twice in the 1928 Scottish Cup Final, both thundering drives from distance as Rangers buried their 25-year-old hoodoo with a 4–0 win over Celtic. Sandy was the longest serving player in the team that memorable day, and having played in the losing finals of 1921 and 1922 victory would have tasted all the sweeter. He would go on to experience defeat again one year later against Kilmarnock but did secure two more winners' medals before the curtain fell on his playing career.

Archibald also won 12 league championship winners' medals, a phenomenal achievement by any reckoning. His was a prolific scoring ratio for a winger, with 168 goals in 661 competitive appearances. Celtic manager Willie Maley once paid him this tribute: "So long as he is on the pitch, we can never be sure of victory over Rangers, no matter the score."

On the international front, Archibald made a somewhat modest eight appearances for Scotland during an era when honours were passed around by the selectors in the less important fixtures against Ireland and Wales. Significantly, half of his caps were won in the biggest fixture of them all – against England.

Archibald had a cheerful disposition, a rare sense of humour, and was often the life-and-soul of the dressing room. It was a sad day for the club when he retired from playing in 1934. In November that same year he was appointed secretary/manager of his old club Raith Rovers, a post he held for five years. In 1939 he moved to Fife rivals Dunfermline Athletic, where he remained manager until his death in November 1946 at the age of just 49.

Sandy Archibald factfile
Born: Aberdour, Fife, 6th September 1897
Died: November 1946
Appearances: 661
Goals: 168
Full international appearances while at Rangers: 8 caps for Scotland

Honours:

League championship: 1917/18, 1919/20, 1920/21, 1922/23, 1923/24, 1924/25, 1926/27, 1927/28, 1928/29, 1929/30, 1930/31, 1932/33

Scottish FA Cup: 1928, 1930, 1932

Glasgow Cup: 1917/18, 1921/22, 1922/23, 1923/24, 1924/25, 1929/30, 1932/33, 1933/34

Glasgow Merchants' Charity Cup: 1919, 1922, 1923, 1925, 1928, 1929, 1930, 1931, 1932

Lord Provost's Rent Relief Fund Cup: 1921/22

— FOR KING AND COUNTRY —

Rangers players, past or present, who served with distinction in the armed forces during the Great War included:

Dr James A Paterson: Captain, 14th battalion, London Regiment, London Scottish

Andrew N Cunningham: Second lieutenant, gunner, Royal Field Artillery

James Eadie Gordon: Sergeant, Highland Light Infantry

Willie Reid: Gunner, Royal Field Artillery, 52nd Lowland Division

Frederick B Gray: Second lieutenant, 9th battalion, Cameronians (Scottish Rifles)

James Hamilton Speirs: Second lieutenant, 7th battalion, Cameron Highlanders, 15th Scottish Division

James Hill Galt: Second lieutenant, Argyll & Sutherland Highlanders

John Fleming: Corporal, 8th battalion, Cameron Highlanders

John Clarke: Rifleman, 16th (Pioneer) battalion, Royal Irish Rifles (36th Ulster Division)

Thomas Allan Muirhead: Second lieutenant, 1st/2nd battalion, King's Own Scottish Borderers

David B Murray: Private, 8th battalion, Seaforth

Highlanders, 15th Scottish Division

Dr Thomas A Gilchrist: 1st/2nd battalion, Argyll and Sutherland Highlanders

Finlay Speedie: Private, Argyll and Sutherland Highlanders

Scott Duncan: Signalling instructor, Royal Field Artillery

Jimmy Low: Second lieutenant, 6th battalion, Seaforth Highlanders

Alex Barrie: Corporal, 2nd battalion, Highland Light Infantry

Tom McDonald: Royal Horse Artillery

John McKeown Bovill: Rifleman, Royal Irish Rifles

Sandy Archibald: Stationed at the Curragh Camp, County Kildare

Dr William F Kivlichan: Lieutenant, Royal Army Medical Corps, attached to the King's Own African Rifles

Alex Bennett: Cameronians, Scottish Rifles

John Bertram Jackson: Royal Scots Fusiliers

George Turner Livingstone: Royal Army Medical Corps

David Taylor: Royal Field Artillery

Walter Daniel John Tull: Second lieutenant, 5th battalion, Middlesex Regiment

John Rankin: Royal Army Medical Corps

R Smith: Mechanic, Royal Flying Corps

David Brown and Jock Buchanan were both army sergeants whilst Tom Sinclair and James Young also served in the British Army. John McCulloch, George Dickson and Jimmy Lister also served in the Armed Forces.

The above list should not of course be considered all inclusive, and it is to be regretted that full service details are not available for all of the above players.

— RANGERS LEGENDS: DAVID MEIKLEJOHN (1919–37) —

David Meiklejohn: Rangers' greatest ever captain?

There have been many great captains of Rangers throughout the club's history, and perhaps the greatest of them all was David Meiklejohn.

Born in Govan in the last days of the 19th century, 'Meik' signed for Rangers from Maryhill Juniors in August 1919. He would go on to play 635 games for the Light Blues, winning no fewer than 12 league championship and five Scottish Cup winners' medals.

A wing half or centre half, he was an inspiring player of great class and composure, strength and resolution with a never-say-die attitude. A man of immense presence, Meiklejohn was a true leader of men.

His huge importance to the Rangers team of the time was never more clearly illustrated than in the 1925/26 season, when injury restricted him to just 12 league games of a possible 38. Rangers subsequently finished in sixth position – the lowest ever for the club. Moreover, it was the only campaign during a nine-year sequence in which Rangers failed to win the title – and in each of the other eight seasons Meiklejohn had played at least 30 games.

His finest match was surely the 1928 Scottish Cup Final. With club captain Tommy Muirhead absent through injury, it fell to David Meiklejohn to lead the Ibrox men against great rivals Celtic, fully aware that the club had not enjoyed success in the competition for a quarter of a century. Goalless at the interval, it was clear that the opening goal would be critical. Ten minutes into the second half Alan Morton's cross was volleyed goalwards by Jimmy Fleming. Celtic goalkeeper John Thomson was beaten, only for the ball to be punched off the line by Parkhead defender Willie McStay. 'Meik' proved to be a true leader as he stepped forward to take the spot kick ahead of regular penalty-taker Bob McPhail. His aim was true and thereafter Rangers played like men possessed as the cup hoodoo was dispersed to the four winds. McPhail made it 2–0 before two long-range pile-drivers from Sandy Archibald completed the rout.

At the post-match banquet 'Meik' told his teammates, "We have won it at last – we can win it again." His words proved to be prophetic as Rangers went on to win the Scottish Cup five times in the next eight years . . .

In an international career spanning 11 years from 1922 to 1933 Meiklejohn played 15 times for Scotland, captaining his country twice against England. One of the true giants of the inter-war years, he was later paid the following tribute by then Celtic chairman Bob Kelly: "Davie Meiklejohn was the greatest Rangers player of all . . . he was a most inspiring captain. No centre half before his time or since has headed the ball

constructively right and left to his wing-halves more regularly
and skillfully. He was a magnificent captain and a true football
master."

Meiklejohn was manager of Partick Thistle from 1949 until
his death ten years later at the age of just 58, collapsing at
Broomfield Park, Airdrie at the end of a League Cup fixture.
His passing was mourned by all friends of Rangers and by
football lovers across the globe.

David Meiklejohn factfile
Born: Govan, 12th December 1900
Died: 22nd August 1959
Appearances: 635
Goals: 52
Full international appearances while at Rangers: 15 caps for
Scotland
Honours:
League championship: 1920/21, 1922/23, 1923/24, 1924/25,
1926/27,1927/28, 1928/29, 1929/30, 1930/31, 1932/33, 1933/34,
1934/35
Scottish FA Cup: 1928, 1930, 1932, 1934, 1936
Glasgow Cup: 1921/22, 1923/24, 1924/25, 1929/30, 1931/32,
1932/33, 1933/34, 1935/36
Glasgow Merchants' Charity Cup: 1922, 1923, 1925, 1928,
1929, 1930, 1931, 1932, 1934

— GREAT EUROPEAN NIGHTS AT IBROX 2 —

Rangers 4	Red Star Bratislava 3
McMillan	Scherer 2
Scott	Dolinsky
Wilson	
Millar	

1959/60 European Cup, second round, first leg
11th November 1959
Attendance: 80,000

After overwhelming Anderlecht in the opening round, Rangers were drawn to play in Eastern Europe for the very first time in European competition. The destination was the beautiful city of Bratislava.

The Cold War was at its height with Bratislava in 1959 the second city of Czechoslovakia, under Communist occupation behind the Iron Curtain that split Europe in two from 1945 to 1990. The opposition were Ruda Hvezda (Red Star) or CH Bratislava – today known as Inter Bratislava. The Czechoslovakian champions had defeated Porto (home and away) in the previous round.

A packed Ibrox witnessed a sensational opening when Ian McMillan opened the scoring from 16 yards from an Alex Scott cross after just 90 seconds, only for the game to degenerate into a kicking match as the visitors quickly identified Scott as the danger man – body-checking, tripping and harassing him at every opportunity.

Red Star turned the match on its head when Adolf Scherer (one of four Czech internationals in their team) equalised after 16 minutes, then on the half-hour Milan Dolinsky put the visitors ahead. They were an accomplished, skilful side who were controlling the tempo of the game.

The game had been simmering throughout the opening 45 minutes, and exploded on the cusp of the interval when a mazy run on the left by Davie Wilson ended with a cross that led to Sammy Baird colliding in mid-air with goalkeeper Frantisek Hlavaty, the loose ball falling to Scott who lobbed it into the unguarded net with the goalkeeper lying prostrate on the penalty spot.

Swiss referee Daniel Mellet awarded the goal to the fury of the visitors, and with their goalkeeper stretchered off after a considerable delay it fell to Dezider Cimra to replace him in goal in the days before substitutions.

The drama was far from over. Before the interval Red Star were reduced to nine men when Sammy Baird was felled by a wild kick from Jiri Tichy. Mayhem ensued, and amidst the confusion Stefan Matlak was ordered off.

After the interval Hlavaty resumed between the posts with his head heavily bandaged. The visitors regained the lead after 68 minutes when, after a period of sustained Rangers pressure a lightning-quick counter-attack took full advantage of a Johnny Little slip, Dolinsky crossing for Scherer to net at the culmination of a slick-passing move that had encompassed virtually the full length of the park.

It had been Red Star's first attack of the second half, and the Scottish champions were quick to respond. Five minutes after falling behind they were awarded a penalty when Baird, who revelled in games against continental opposition and Celtic alike, was sent sprawling.

The spot kick was a drama in itself, a line of defenders indulging in excessive gamesmanship by standing in front of Eric Caldow as he prepared to take the penalty. They danced around the ball, pointing at it and then at the corner flag, and when order was eventually restored the distraction had worked, for Hlavaty, with a dive to the left, diverted the full back's effort wide for a corner.

The Light Blues would not be denied, however. Sixty seconds later a superb dummy from McMillan wrong-footed the Red Star defence before 'the Wee Prime Minister' crossed for Davie Wilson to hook in the equaliser.

Fully aware that the second leg awaited in Bratislava, Rangers went all out for the winner. Baird missed two good chances, and a momentous game looked certain to finish all square, until the final minute when Jimmy Millar grabbed the winner following a neat Scott-McMillan move.

Rangers progressed to the quarter-finals for the first time following a 1-1 draw in the second leg.

Rangers team: Niven; Caldow, Little; Davis, Telfer, Stevenson; Scott, McMillan, Millar, Baird, Wilson

— BRAND TO THE FORE —

Rangers striker Ralph Brand was joint top scorer in the inaugural European Cup Winners' Cup in 1960/61 along with Fiorentina's Kurt Hamrin. Both players netted five goals in the tournament, with Hamrin equalling Brand's tally with a goal in his side's 4–1 aggregate victory over Rangers in the final.

— RANGERS' TRIPLE CROWNS: 1964 —

The great Rangers team of the early 1960s had won two of the three national tournaments in each of the preceding three years, accumulating six out of a possible nine trophies – but the Triple Crown, as it was known in those days, had eluded them somehow or other on each occasion. Not so in season 1963/64 – as the side of Jim Baxter, Ian McMillan, Jimmy Millar, Ralph Brand and Davie Wilson reached its peak in glorious fashion.

To the delight of the Rangers fans, great rivals Celtic were defeated five times out of five during the campaign. However, the main challenge in the league championship race came from Kilmarnock who, alongside Dundee, had represented the greatest threat to Ibrox throughout the previous three campaigns. Rangers' home form was somewhat patchy with Hearts, St Johnstone and St Mirren all scoring three goals (and winning in the process). A certain Alex Ferguson scored three goals for St Johnstone in a 3–2 win at Ibrox on 21st December 1963. Nonetheless, the title was won by six points from the Ayrshire men with the clinching fixture being a 2–0 home win over Dundee United two games from the tape.

The League Cup saw Rangers top a section that included both Kilmarnock and Celtic, securing 11 points out of a possible 12. The final attracted the first six-figure attendance in the competition's history with 105,607 spectators present as Rangers overwhelmed Division Two side Morton 5–0 with Jim Forrest netting four, ensuring a place in the history books as the only player in British football history to score four in a major cup final. The Greenock side had caught the public's imagination with an exciting run to Hampden that had seen both Motherwell and Hibernian eliminated – but they were no match for the Light Blues in the final.

The Scottish FA Cup came alive in the third round when an Ibrox audience of 62,000 saw Partick Thistle defeated 3–0, then in the last eight Celtic's visit to Govan produced a comfortable 2–0 home win before 84,724 spectators. The final was an absolute classic, regarded by many of those present as the finest of them all – even today, 44 years on. Rangers defeated Dundee 3–1 with two goals from Jimmy Millar and one from Ralph Brand in front of a 120,982 crowd.

The European Cup provided the opportunity of a fourth trophy, but it was not to be. Rangers were severely handicapped by injury to several experienced players as they lost to the great Real Madrid side of the era in the first round.

Leading appearance makers: Billy Ritchie and John Greig, 52 games (ever-presents)
Leading goalscorer: Jim Forrest, 39 goals

— RANGERS LEGENDS: ALAN MORTON (1920–33) —

Alan Morton is an iconic name in the history of Rangers Football Club and of Scottish football. One of the greatest players to appear for the club, Morton's standing in Ibrox folklore is illustrated by the fact that a portrait in oils of the winger stands at the top of the marble staircase inside the stadium. As well as his legendary status at Rangers, he was also one of the finest talents ever to wear the famous black-and-white hoops of Queen's Park.

Born in 1893 in Partick, the son of a coalmaster, Morton was educated at Airdrie Academy. In 1913 he signed for Queen's Park, where his brother Bob was centre forward. He would stay at Hampden for seven years before turning professional with Rangers in 1920 after having played 248 games for the amateurs.

Morton was new manager Bill Struth's first signing – and he surely never made a better one, despite serving as Ibrox boss for fully 34 years. Standing just five feet four inches tall and weighing little more than nine stone, Morton's remarkable talent nonetheless made him a giant of the game. His first touch and dribbling skills were unmatched, while his pace and balance gave him an uncanny ability to change direction. Morton was naturally right-footed, and as the vast majority of his games in the blue of Rangers saw him line up at outside left this enabled him to cut inside the full back almost at will. He was also famed for the floating cross that seemed to almost hang over the goalmouth, inviting a headed goal.

The great Alan Morton

Morton played almost 500 games for Rangers, winning nine league championship winners' medals. He received a total of 31 international caps for Scotland (the first two whilst still an amateur with Queen's), a record that stood for two decades until overtaken by another Ibrox legend, George Young. He first received international recognition when selected for three of the four Victory Internationals at the end of the First World War. Morton played 11 times against England between 1921 and 1932 – most famously in the 1928 'Wembley Wizards' game when the Scots won 5–1. It was during this game that he attained the nickname for which he is known to this day, 'the Wee Blue Devil', given to him by an exasperated English fan as he tortured and tormented full backs Frederick Goodall and Harry Jones and provided crosses for all three of Alex Jackson's goals.

That fan's remark was reported and the nickname caught on with the wider football public, but at Ibrox he was always known as 'the Wee Society Man' – a testament to his immaculate attire of waistcoat, spats and bowler hat.

By profession a mining engineer, Morton practiced his trade throughout his football career. When he retired from the game in 1933 at the age of 40 he was immediately appointed a club director – the only man in the club's history to move directly from dressing room to boardroom. He remained a director until shortly before his death on 15th December 1971, the same day as another Rangers legend, Torry Gillick, passed away.

The Wee Society Man or the Wee Blue Devil – take your pick. Whatever he was known as, Alan Morton was an all-time Rangers great.

Alan Morton factfile
Born: Partick, 24th April 1893
Died: 15th December 1971
Appearances: 498
Goals: 119
Full international appearances while at Rangers: 29 caps for Scotland
Honours:
League championship: 1920/21, 1922/23, 1923/24, 1924/25, 1926/27, 1927/28, 1928/29, 1929/30, 1930/31
Scottish FA Cup: 1928, 1930
Glasgow Cup: 1922/23, 1923/24, 1924/25, 1929/30, 1931/32
Glasgow Merchants' Charity Cup: 1922, 1923, 1925, 1928, 1929, 1931
Lord Provost's Rent Relief Fund Cup: 1921/22

— FANCY A GAME? —

Of current Scottish league clubs Rangers have yet to play either Airdrie United or 2008/09 newcomers Annan in any competition.

— ONE DAY, TWO GAMES —

During the First World War, concerns about absenteeism from essential services led to a ban on midweek football except on public holidays. This measure created such problems with fixture congestion in 1917 that many clubs agreed to play two fixtures on the one day in order that the league season might end on the scheduled date of 28th April.

So, on 21st April, Rangers played both Hamilton (a 3.30pm kick-off) and Queens Park (6.45pm). It proved to be a day of mixed fortunes for the club, Rangers losing 3–1 at Douglas Park, Hamilton before beating Queen's Park (who had won 2–0 at Partick Thistle in the afternoon) 1–0 at Ibrox. Both of Rangers' games attracted 7,000 spectators and seven players turned out in both games for the club: Lock, Manderson, Blair, Lawson, Cairns, Bowie, and Anderson.

— EUROPEAN FINALS: CUP WINNERS' CUP, 1961 —

Rangers became the first British club to play in a European final when they defeated Ferencváros, Borussia Mönchengladbach and Wolverhampton Wanderers in the inaugural European Cup Winners' Cup tournament. In the final, they faced the formidable barrier of Italian aces Fiorentina over two legs.

Minus the crucial influence of Jimmy Millar, Rangers were confronted by a cynical display of body-checking and blatant obstruction throughout the first leg at Ibrox as the Florence side displayed the dark side of Italian football. 80,000 spectators looked on aghast as a basic error in defence presented Gianfranco Petris with a clear opening when Harold Davis's backpass fell woefully short of Billy Ritchie, the Italian presenting his colleague Luigi Milan with a simple chance to open the scoring. Seven minutes later Rangers had a golden opportunity to equalise when they were awarded a penalty as Alberto Orzan swept the feet from Ian McMillan as he weaved his way through the Fiorentina defence. A heated debate followed on the merits of the award between the referee and an Italian coach, not to mention several Fiorentina players, but when the dust had settled Eric Caldow sent the ball well wide of goal with custodian Enrico Albertosi prancing about on the six-yard line! No retake was ordered, and Rangers spent the rest of the evening in frenzied attack, throwing high ball after high ball into a packed defence to no avail, and the die seemed cast in the closing seconds when a muddle between Davis and Shearer presented Milan with a second goal after a one-two with Swedish winger Kurt Hamrin.

In later years Eric Caldow would rate Hamrin as second only to Gento in assessing the quality of wingers he had faced, and Rangers would have cause to remember his name after the return in Florence. With Millar restored to the ranks for the Saturday evening fixture, Rangers had every reason for renewed optimism and almost struck an early blow only for the chance to be spurned by Davie Wilson. The miss proved even more costly when, after 12 minutes, Milan chested home a Hamrin cross after the Swede had eluded both Baxter and Caldow.

The Scots at last breached the Florentine defence on the hour when Alex Scott blasted home an 18-yard volley after Ralph Brand's shot was blocked by a defender. Inspired by this strike, Rangers piled on the pressure with Millar coming perilously close to adding a second and a strong penalty appeal denied when Scott was bowled over, but with the sands of time running out a breakaway by Hamrin saw the winger evade three Rangers defenders on the right, cut along the goal line and crash home a magnificent shot from a tight angle before falling spread-eagled amongst the photographers. At the end Rangers received a standing ovation from the 50,000 spectators in the Stadio Comunale, but to the Italians went the spoils of victory and their fans lit bonfires on the darkened terraces as their heroes embarked on a lap of honour to celebrate their triumph.

European Cup Winners' Cup Final, first leg
Wednesday 17th May 1961, Ibrox Stadium
Rangers 0 Fiorentina 2 (Milan 2)
Attendance: 80,000
Rangers team: Ritchie; Shearer, Caldow; Davis, Paterson, Baxter; Wilson, McMillan, Scott, Brand, Hume

European Cup Winners' Cup Final, second leg
Saturday 27th May 1961
Stadio Comunale, Florence
Fiorentina 2 (Milan, Hamrin) Rangers 1 (Scott)
Attendance: 50,000
Rangers team: Ritchie; Shearer, Caldow; Davis, Paterson,
Baxter; Scott, McMillan, Millar, Brand, Wilson

— RANGERS MANAGERS: BILL STRUTH (1920–54) —

The longest serving and most successful of Ibrox managers, Bill
Struth served as trainer under William Wilton from 1914 before
succeeding him in 1920. Born in Milnathort, Kinross-shire in
1875, his sporting background was in athletics rather than
football, but before joining the club he had worked for both
Hearts and Clyde as trainer.

Struth served as manager for fully 30 years, during which time
Rangers secured a staggering trophy count in excess of 80 –
including no fewer than 25 league championships, establishing
the club beyond question as the dominant force in Scottish football
between the wars. Remarkably, in both 1929/30 and 1933/34 the
club won every competition it entered. A strict disciplinarian,
Struth ruled Ibrox with an iron fist. Not a tactician in the accepted
modern understanding, he delegated that responsibility, as with
all managers of the time, to his senior players. He was elected
to the board in 1947, finally retired as manager in 1954, and
remained a director until his death in 1956, aged 81.

Bill Struth's honours:
League championship: 1920/21,1922/23, 1923/24, 1924/25,
1926/27, 1927/28, 1928/29, 1929/30, 1930/31, 1932/33,
1933/34, 1934/35, 1936/37, 1938/39, 1939/40, 1940/41,
1941/42, 1942/43, 1943/44, 1944/45, 1945/46, 1946/47,
1948/49, 1949/50, 1952/53
Scottish Cup: 1928, 1930, 1932, 1934, 1935, 1936, 1948,
1949, 1950, 1953
Scottish League Cup: 1946/47, 48/49
Glasgow Cup: 1921/22, 1922/23, 1923/24, 1924/25, 1929/30,

1931/32, 1932/33, 1933/34, 1935/36, 1936/37, 1937/38,
1939/40, 1941/42, 1942/43, 1943/44, 1944/45, 1947/48,
1949/50, 1953/54
Glasgow Merchants' Charity Cup: 1922, 1923, 1925, 1928,
1929, 1930, 1931, 1932, 1933, 1934, 1939, 1940, 1941, 1942,
1944, 1945, 1946, 1947, 1948, 1951
Lord Provost's' Rent Relief Fund Cup: 1921/22
Scottish Emergency War Cup: 1940
Southern League Cup: 1940/41,19 41/42, 1942/43, 1944/45
Summer Cup: 1942
Scottish Victory Cup: 1946

— UP FOR THE CUP —

With 33 Scottish Cup wins to their name Rangers are well within
sight of Celtic's record of 34 victories. Rangers' triumphs in the
final have come against the following clubs:

Opponents	Victories	Years
Celtic	7	1894, 1928, 1963, 1966, 1973, 1999, 2002
Aberdeen	4	1953, 1978, 1993, 2000
Hearts	3	1903, 1976, 1996
Kilmarnock	3	1898, 1932, 1960
Dundee	2	1964, 2003
St Mirren	2	1934, 1962
Airdrieonians	1	1992
Clyde	1	1949
Dumbarton	1	1897
Dundee United	1	1981
East Fife	1	1950
Hamilton	1	1935
Hibernian	1	1979
Morton	1	1948
Partick Thistle	1	1930
Queen of the South	1	2008
Third Lanark	1	1936
Falkirk	1	2009

— RANGERS LEGENDS: DOUGIE GRAY (1925–47) —

Dougie Gray: 945 games in a Rangers shirt

"Gray was just Gray" was a constant feature of Rangers match reports between the wars. Douglas Gray was a model of consistency, the quality of his performances taken as read. A full back signed from Aberdeen Muggiemoss in June 1925, he served fully 22 years at Ibrox, making him the longest serving player in the club's history.

He had succeeded another legendary figure at full back – the Ulsterman Bert Manderson who had captained the Light Blues during years of success. Comfortable with the ball on either foot, Gray was renowned for both his anticipation in the tackle and his distribution. Famous for his longevity and noted for goal-line clearances, he was known as "the best goalkeeper Rangers never had". Not the most adventurous of full backs, he scored just two goals (both from the penalty spot in 1930/31) for the club in his long career.

When he made his debut on 3rd October 1925 in a 3–0 home league win over Kilmarnock he could number Willie Robb, Arthur Dixon, Tommy Muirhead, Sandy Archibald and Andy Cunningham amongst his teammates. Two decades later in his final outing in Light Blue he played alongside Jock Shaw, George Young, Scot Symon, Willie Waddell, Torry Gillick and Jimmy Smith – legends all.

Gray's 945 appearances for the club (encompassing all games) may never be broken, and the same can surely be said of his record 16 league championships (including those won in wartime). In terms of league appearances his club record of 667 surpasses his nearest rival (Sandy Archibald) by in excess of 150. In addition he won six Scottish Cup winners' medals, including the historic 1928 triumph when Celtic were overcome 4–0 to secure the club's first success in the competition for fully 25 years. Indeed he was an ever-present that season as the club secured the league and cup double for the first time. When the club won three consecutive Scottish Cups for the first time from 1934 to 1936 he played in all 20 ties. His career total of 49 first-team winners' medals is as staggering as it is unbeatable. He also played ten times for Scotland – a considerable tally for the time.

In the twilight of his career Gray was part of the Rangers squad that remarkably flew to Hanover, Germany in October 1945 (in the wake of the cessation of hostilities) to play a Combined Services XI. After retiring as a player two years later, he had a spell as a coach with Clyde.

Douglas Gray factfile
Born: Alford, Aberdeenshire, 4th April 1905; Died: 1972
Appearances: 889
Goals: 2
Full international appearances while at Rangers: 10 caps for Scotland
Honours:
League championship: 1926/27, 1927/28, 1928/29, 1929/30, 1930/31, 1932/33, 1933/34, 1934/35, 1936/37, 1938/39, 1939/40,

1940/41, 1941/42, 1942/43, 1943/44, 1944/45
Scottish FA Cup: 1928, 1930, 1932, 1934, 1935, 1936
Scottish Emergency War Cup: 1940
Southern League Cup: 1940/41, 1941/42, 1942/43
Summer Cup: 1942
Glasgow Cup: 1929/30, 1931/32, 1932/33, 1933/34, 1935/36, 1936/37, 1937/38, 1939/40, 1941/42, 1942/43, 1943/44, 1944/45
Glasgow Merchants Charity Cup: 1928, 1929, 1931, 1932, 1933, 1934, 1940, 1941, 1942, 1944

— GREAT EUROPEAN NIGHTS AT IBROX 3 —

Rangers 2   **Tottenham Hotspur 3**
Brand   Smith 2
Wilson   Greaves

1962/63 European Cup Winners' Cup, second round, second leg
11th December 1962
Attendance: 80,000

Eighteen months after beating Wolves in the semi-final of the European Cup Winners' Cup Rangers found themselves in another 'Battle of Britain' encounter in the same competition. This time their opponents were Tottenham Hotspur, who boasted a multi-talented outfit that had become the first club in the 20th century to win the league and cup double two years earlier. Defensive errors cost Rangers dear in the first leg at White Hart Lane, Spurs winning 5–2.

Ibrox hopes of salvaging the tie were killed stone-dead in the return, when Jimmy Greaves scored a wonder goal after eight minutes when he strode through the home defence following a flick by Bobby Smith almost on the halfway line, and ghosted past Harold Davis, Ronnie McKinnon and Eric Caldow. It was one of the greatest goals ever seen at Ibrox, and it silenced the old ground. Ralphie Brand headed the equaliser from a Willie Henderson cross in 47 minutes, the culmination of a move started by Caldow deep in his own half, but within three minutes Smith put his side back in front from a John White pass. Rangers fought back once again, with the capacity crowd roaring them on. Brand struck the crossbar, then Davie Wilson's 74th minute free kick levelled matters again. The home side pressed for the third goal that would at least salvage some pride on the night. Undeservedly, however, when the goal did come in the last minute it was Smith's header from a Dave Mackay cross that won the game.

Tottenham had been worthy winners over the two legs, but they demonstrated their appreciation of the opposition when they lined up to applaud Rangers off the park at the final whistle. The Londoners went on to become the first British club to win a European trophy, with a convincing 5–1 triumph over Atlético Madrid in Rotterdam.

Rangers team: Ritchie; Shearer, Caldow; Davis, McKinnon, Baxter; Henderson, McMillan, Millar, Brand, Wilson

— ANGLO XI —

A team of Rangers players who all played for England:

1. Chris Woods
2. Gary Stevens
3. Michael Ball
4. Ray Wilkins
5. Terry Butcher
6. Graham Roberts
7. Trevor Steven
8. Paul Gascoigne
9. Mark Hateley
10. Trevor Francis
11. Mark Walters

— RANGERS LEGENDS: JIMMY SMITH (1928–46) —

Jimmy Smith: a fearless competitor

No player in the club's history has scored more goals than Jimmy Smith. His record of 382 competitive goals in 411 games, including 299 league goals in 316 games, represents a phenomenal strike rate by any standards.

Smith, a centre forward with a penchant for scoring goals, signed for Rangers from East Stirlingshire in December 1928 whilst still a pupil at Airdrie Academy, and within three months he was making his first-team debut at the age of just 17. The 1930 close-season tour of North America saw him stake his claim for first-team recognition with 18 goals in just seven games, and in the domestic campaign that followed he justified his selection with 21 goals in as many games.

This was an Ibrox team that was dominating Scottish football as never before. Competition was fierce in a forward line of some considerable talent – Dr James Marshall, Jimmy Fleming, Bob McPhail, Sam English, Torry Gillick and Alex Venters were all vying for places – but Smith's scoring record was one that simply could never be ignored.

Possessing an intimidating physique, Smith was a fearless competitor both on the ground and in the air in an era when the game was much more physical than today. He also possessed a turn of pace, first touch and quality of distribution that belied his build.

In five consecutive seasons from 1932/33 Smith scored in excess of 30 league goals – a remarkable level of consistency. To this day only he and Durie Wilson have scored six goals in a league game for the club. Remarkably, Smith achieved this feat twice: first, in a 9–1 home win over Ayr United in August 1933, then almost exactly a year later in a 7–1 win at Dunfermline.

Perhaps his finest game in Light Blue came on New Year's Day 1936 at Celtic Park when, with the visitors trailing 1–3, Smith displayed outstanding leadership to inspire a memorable fightback to win 4–3, with the winner a superb 84th minute diving header from a Jimmy Fiddes corner.

Dubbed 'the Joker', Smith won 24 winners' medals in an Ibrox career that stretched for 18 years. He was certainly fond of Hampden, where he won three consecutive Scottish Cups from 1934 to 1936, the first time any Rangers side had achieved such a feat. He scored in the 1934 final, twice in 1935 in a 2–1 win over Hamilton Academical, and just for good measure netted the only goal of the 1940 War Cup Final against Dundee United.

In one of his last games as a Ranger he scored against Dynamo Moscow in November 1945 in the famous 2–2 draw at Ibrox that attracted 95,000 spectators.

After his playing career ended Smith continued to serve the club as trainer (1948–56) and chief scout (1956–67).

Jimmy Smith factfile
Born: Airdrie, 24th September 1911
Died: 4th December 2003

Appearances: 411

Goals: 382

Full international appearances while at Rangers: 6 caps for Scotland

Honours:

League championship: 1930/31, 1932/33, 1933/34, 1934/35, 1936/37, 1939/40, 1940/41, 1941/42, 1944/45

Scottish FA Cup: 1934, 1935, 1936

Scottish Emergency War Cup: 1940

Southern League Cup: 1940/41, 1944/45

Glasgow Cup: 1931/32, 1932/33, 1935/36, 1936/37, 1937/38, 1942/43

Glasgow Merchants' Charity Cup: 1931, 1934, 1944

— FINAL ECSTASY AND AGONY —

Rangers' biggest win in a Scottish Cup Final was a 5–0 thrashing of St Mirren at Hampden Park in 1934. The club's biggest defeat in the final came in 1969, when the Light Blues were hammered 4–0 by Jock Stein's then dominant Celtic team.

The club's most emphatic victory in the Scottish League Cup Final was a 5–0 drubbing of Morton in the 1963/64 season. Less memorably, the 'Gers went down 7–1 to Celtic in the final of the same competition in 1957/58.

— EURO GOALFESTS —

Rangers' biggest ever win in European competition was a 10–0 thrashing of Maltese minnows Valetta at Ibrox in the Cup Winners' Cup in 1983. As the 'Gers had already won 8–0 away, the final aggregate score was an incredible 18–0!

Less memorably, Rangers were trounced 12–4 on aggregate by Eintracht Frankfurt in the semi-final of the European Cup in 1960 after 6–1 and 6–3 defeats to the German champions. The club's worst single defeat in Europe, though, was against Spanish giants Real Madrid – a 6–0 drubbing in the Bernabeu in 1963.

— HISTORY OF THE GROUNDS: FIRST IBROX —

There was considerable debate in the sporting press of the day when Rangers announced their intention to move to a new ground at Ibrox. Other south-side locations at Pollokshields and Strathbungo were considered but discarded. Were the Light Blues making a mistake in moving "out of the city into the country"? The district of Ibrox was at the time on the outskirts of the city, but the club rightly anticipated the spread westward of the city's growing population and the extension of Glasgow's transport system.

First Ibrox was situated adjacent to the present stadium, with its eastern boundary in Copland Road, on the site presently occupied by Edmiston House. The ground was advanced for its time, boasting a grandstand seating 1,200 spectators and raised ash terraces that afforded clear views of the field of play. In the north-east corner, by Copland Road, stood a splendid pavilion with dressing rooms and a committee room. A running track was used for the club's popular Annual Sports Meeting that would become a key fixture in the athletics calendar for the next 75 years. The opening fixture at the new ground on 20th August 1887 attracted a staggering (for the time) attendance in excess of 18,000 spectators for the visit of the leading English club of the day, Preston North End, who would go on to win the league and cup double the following season. The attendance that day was at the time the largest recorded gathering to watch any game in the Light Blues' history – indeed it would be another seven years before it was bettered.

It seemed that Rangers had found a ground that would be their home for decades to come, yet by the end of the century they had outgrown First Ibrox. The increasing popularity of the game, the increasing population of the 'Second City of the Empire', and the club's success in the 1890s demanded a grander stage – and so it came to be that the present Ibrox Stadium was developed, adjoining First Ibrox.

— SUCCESS IN THE LEAGUE CUP —

Rangers have won the Scottish League Cup a record 25 times since the competition was formed in 1946. The club's victories in the final have come against the following teams:

Opponents	Victories	Seasons
Celtic	8	1964/65, 1970/71, 1975/76, 1977/78, 1983/84, 1986/87, 1990/91, 2002/03
Aberdeen	5	1946/47, 1978/79, 1987/88, 1988/89, 1992/93
Dundee United	3	1981/82, 1984/85, 2007/08
Hearts	2	1961/62, 1996/97
Ayr United	1	2001/02
Hibernian	1	1993/94
Kilmarnock	1	1960/61
Morton	1	1963/64
Motherwell	1	2004/05
Raith Rovers	1	1948/49
St Johnstone	1	1998/99

— RANGERS' TRIPLE CROWNS: 1976 —

Under the leadership of manager Jock Wallace, Rangers had broken the Jock Stein domination of Scottish football by winning the league championship in season 1974/75, the club's first title in 11 years. The following campaign would be a historic one for the domestic game – for better or worse – with the introduction of the Premier Division. In a league restricted to just ten clubs playing each other four times, competition would now be more intense than ever. The opening day's fixtures included Rangers v Celtic at Ibrox watched by an attendance of 69,594 – a Premier Division record that stands to this day. Rangers started the defence of their title with a 2–1 win courtesy of goals from Derek Johnstone and Quinton Young, with a certain Kenny Dalglish scoring for the visitors, and thus the champions had set out their stall for the domination of the domestic season, remaining unbeaten against their Old Firm rivals for the remainder of the campaign.

The first half of the league season was not without its hiccups with five games lost, but following a 1–0 loss at Pittodrie on 6th December 1975 (the first for ten years) Rangers went through the remainder of the campaign undefeated. In a run of 26 unbeaten games in both league and Scottish Cup the key result, as on so many occasions, was a 1–0 home win over Celtic at Ne'erday with Johnstone again the marksman. Rangers were never to be toppled after achieving the summit following a 2–0 win over Hibernian at Ibrox on 17th January, and ended up winning the title by a margin of six points. The trophy was clinched two games from home with a 1–0 win at Dundee United thanks to a Johnstone goal in the opening minute of the game, while Celtic were suffering defeat to relegation-threatened Ayr United 1–2 at Parkhead.

The League Cup had been won the previous October when a spectacular flying header from Alex MacDonald proved to be the only goal of an Old Firm encounter at Hampden.

The Scottish Cup campaign had come alive in the penultimate round when, on a night of torrential rain in Mount Florida, Rangers came back from the dead and a two-goal deficit against Motherwell to win 3–2. In the final against Hearts the Ibrox men were easy 3–1 winners with Derek Johnstone – one week after his first-minute strike at Tannadice – again finding the net with a header in the opening minute from a Tommy McLean free kick. Somewhat bizarrely, referee Bobby Davidson had started proceedings three minutes early, so the opening goal arrived before the scheduled kick-off!

In the European Cup Rangers eliminated Bohemians Dublin in the opening round before losing in both legs to French champions St Etienne, an accomplished side who went on to reach the Hampden final before succumbing to Bayern Munich as the West Germans clinched a third successive European Cup.

Leading appearance maker: John Greig, 55 games (ever-present)
Leading goalscorer: Derek Johnstone, 31 goals

— RANGERS LEGENDS: WILLIE THORNTON
(1936–54) —

Willie Thornton: "Wore the Light Blue to the honour of himself and the club he served"

Willie Thornton was a thorough gentleman off the field of play, and a true sportsman on it – a stylish and skilful centre forward whose career record of 247 goals in 410 games is impressive by any reckoning.

He joined Rangers in March 1936, one of three young Willies signed in the late 1930s who would go on to have great careers in Light Blue – the others being Willie Woodburn and Willie Waddell. After making his first-team debut at the age of just 16 in January 1937, Thornton went on to win the first of five league championship winners' medals in 1938/39.

Like other players of his generation, his career was savagely interrupted by the outbreak of war in September 1939. He served with the Duke of Atholl's Highlanders in the Italian campaign, seeing action in Tripoli and Sicily, in unforgettable battles at Anzio and Monte Cassino. In action in Sicily on 18th November 1943 he was awarded the Military Medal.

Back in civvy street, Thornton became a key member of the defensively strong post-war Ibrox team that became known as the 'Iron Curtain' side, much to the centre forward's displeasure. "Of course, we did manage to score the odd goal," he once reflected, and that they did, for his combination with Willie Waddell on the right wing was a potent attacking force with the winger's power, pace and precise cross providing ammunition for the powerful Thornton.

He was the first Rangers player in the post-war era to score 100 league goals, and was a key member of the Ibrox side that clinched Scotland's inaugural Triple Crown in 1948/49, netting 23 goals in 29 appearances including three on the final day of the season in a title-clinching 4–1 win at Albion Rovers.

There were also memorable games and goals in the Scottish Cup as for the second time in the club's history three successive triumphs were secured. In 1948 a trademark Waddell/Thornton combination provided the only goal of a titanic semi-final struggle with Hibernian at Hampden before a colossal 143,570 attendance. In 1949 his hat-trick of headers overwhelmed East Fife in another Hampden semi, and one year later against the same opposition he headed another two goals in a 3–0 final win.

Thornton retired in 1954 and went straight into management with Dundee, enjoying great success in the development of young players of the calibre of Jim Gabriel, Alan Gilzean, Andy Penman and Ian Ure – all of whom went on to play for Scotland. Five years later he succeeded David Meiklejohn at Partick Thistle following his untimely passing, and led them to third place in the league in 1962/63. He returned to Ibrox in September 1968 as assistant to manager David White and remained in the post under successive managers until he retired.

In 1986 the first hospitality suite was opened at Ibrox, and it was only fitting that it was named after Thornton. A portrait of the player was hung in the suite, bearing the inscription "One who wore the Light Blue to the honour of himself and the club he served". Until his death in 1991 he remained involved behind the scenes, looking after the trophy room and as matchday host in the suite that bore his name.

Willie Thornton factfile
Born: Winchburgh, West Lothian, 3rd March 1920
Died: 26th August 1991
Appearances: 410
Goals: 247
Full international appearances while at Rangers: 7 caps for Scotland
Honours:
League championship: 1938/39, 1939/40, 1946/47, 1948/49, 1949/50
Scottish FA Cup: 1948, 1949, 1950
Scottish League Cup: 1946/47, 1948/49
Scottish Emergency War Cup: 1940
Southern League Cup: 1940/41
Summer Cup: 1942
Scottish Victory Cup: 1946
Glasgow Cup: 1939/40, 1947/48, 1949/50
Glasgow Merchants' Charity Cup: 1939, 1940, 1946, 1947, 1948, 1951
Player of the Year: 1952

— SHOOTING STARS —

In 1915 Rangers trainer (and later manager) Bill Struth formed a Rifle Club at Ibrox. Members included Alex Craig, Tommy Cairns, James Bowie, Alex Bennett, Peter Pursell, Scott Duncan, Jimmy Gordon, James Logan and Herbert Lock.

— GREAT EUROPEAN NIGHTS AT IBROX 4 —

Rangers 0 Real Madrid 1

1963/64 European Cup, first round, first leg
25th September 1963
Attendance: 81,215

In the early 1960s no club provided more glamorous opposition than the great Real Madrid. When Rangers drew the Spanish giants in the opening round of season 1963/64 a full house was guaranteed, so much so that the Rangers' directors controversially increased admission prices with the terracing being set at ten shillings. The increase in admission charges did not deter a near-capacity crowd of 81,215 thus setting a precedent of increased prices for decades to come.

Veteran superstars Alfredo di Stefano, Ferenc Puskás and Francisco Gento were all still in the Madrid ranks, although the visitors were arguably not quite as strong as they had been in their heyday when they won five consecutive European Cups between 1956 and 1960.

Rangers were well on top throughout the Ibrox game without being able to penetrate the packed Real defence. Ralph Brand shot into the side-netting from a Davie Wilson cutback after 12 minutes, and struck the inside of a post with a back-header in the second half – but chances were few and far between with goalkeeper José Araquistáin dominant throughout. The Spanish champions remained composed and unbowed however, orchestrated by the peerless di Stefano. The only goal of the game arrived on 87 minutes, a classic strike from 'the Galloping Major' Puskás who started the move in his own half with a sweeping pass to Gento out on the left. The Real captain sped down the wing before curling a cross around Shearer for Puskás to meet on the volley from the edge of the box, the ball flashing past Billy Ritchie and into the net.

Even before that late blow the second leg in Madrid was always going to be a tough proposition. And so it proved, as Rangers were hammered 6–0 by a rampant Real in the Bernabeu.

Rangers team: Ritchie; Shearer, Provan; Greig, McKinnon, Baxter; Henderson, McLean, Forrest, Brand, Wilson

— CONFUSED NATIONALITY —

Rangers players who were born in one country but played for another:

Player	Born	Played for
Andy Goram	England	Scotland
Terry Butcher	Singapore	England
Colin Jackson	England	Scotland
Jimmy Nicholl	Canada	Northern Ireland
Richard Gough	Sweden	Scotland
Stuart McCall	England	Scotland
Brian Laudrup	Austria	Denmark
Brahim Hemdani	France	Algeria

— LOSING THE FIZZ —

One Rangers fan in Kaunas for the Champions League game in 2008 had not had the best of trips. Separated from his luggage for fully 36 hours courtesy of KLM, he had of course endured one of the worst results in the club's history with elimination at the hands of FBK Kaunas.

Checking out of his hotel at noon the day after the game, and feeling thoroughly miserable, he was confronted with a hotel bill that included a bottle of champagne from the mini-bar in his room.

He had drunk only mineral water, and, pointing this out to the hotel receptionist, he strongly emphasised;

"What reason exactly would I have had to have been drinking champagne?"

The champagne was removed from the bill . . .

— RANGERS LEGENDS: GEORGE YOUNG (1941–57) —

George Young: A Rangers colossus

George Young was a true colossus in Rangers' history and one of the club's greatest ever captains.

He signed for Rangers in September 1941 from Kirkintilloch Rob Roy and, after breaking into the first team within three months, was virtually a mainstay thereafter. Rangers dominated wartime football, sweeping all before them, and in the decade that followed the cessation of hostilities Young was a key member of the legendary 'Iron Curtain' defence that was the foundation stone for the Ibrox success of the era.

A truly outstanding defender, at either right back or central defence, he accrued 34 first-team winners' medals during a competitive era when Rangers were challenged by Hibs, Hearts,

Dundee, Motherwell and Aberdeen as well as Celtic. He also played 53 international games for Scotland (plus three wartime), all but five of them as captain – a record that stands to this day. He played five times at Wembley, winning in 1949 and 1951.

Young made the right-back position his own, even if most observers believed that centre half was his true calling – he was fielded at full back to accommodate the outstanding Willie Woodburn in central defence. A true sportsman and a real gentleman on and off the field of play, the gentle giant was never ordered off and was booked just once during his remarkable career – and that caution was for speaking up in defence of teammate Sammy Cox.

He played in the legendary 8–1 league victory over Celtic in January 1943, even scoring two goals in the process – one a penalty, the other a free kick from all of 50 yards! Following the 1948 Scottish Cup triumph over Morton a waiter at the post-match banquet presented George with a champagne cork for good luck. The Ranger carried it with him from that day – and was thereafter known as 'Corky'. He remains the only player to score two penalties in a Scottish Cup Final – the 4–1 win over Clyde in 1949. Four years later in the final against Aberdeen he donned the goalkeeper's jersey when George Niven was injured. The game ended all square at 1–1, with Rangers winning the replay 1–0.

In his final season as a player Young experienced European competitive football – playing in both legs against French champions Nice, but crucially missing the 3–1 play-off defeat in Paris through injury.

He retired in 1957, and at the start of the following season Rangers lost their opening three home league fixtures as well as suffering a catastrophic League Cup Final defeat. Who said one man never made a team?

Corky subsequently went into football management with Third Lanark – and did a first-class job at the cash-strapped club, building an exciting, skilful side which finished third in the league in 1960/61. Some of those who played under him rated Young as good a man manager and tactician as Jock Stein. However, he resigned as manager in December 1962 when former director Bill Hiddlestone regained control, with Young predicting that he would destroy the Hi-Hi. Sadly, within five years he was proven correct as the club was dissolved in the courts.

Young never returned to the game, concentrating on his business as a hotelier, but he was always fondly remembered by football lovers everywhere.

George Young factfile
Born: Grangemouth, Stirlingshire, 27th October 1922
Died: 10th January 1997
Appearances: 664
Goals: 62
Full international appearances while at Rangers: 53 caps for Scotland
Honours:
League championship: 1942/43, 1943/44, 1944/45, 1946/47, 1948/49, 1949/50, 1952/53, 1955/56, 1956/57
Scottish FA Cup: 1948, 1949, 1950, 1953
Scottish League Cup: 1946/47, 1948/49
Southern League Cup: 1941/42, 1942/43, 1944/45
Summer Cup: 1942
Scottish Victory Cup: 1946
Glasgow Cup: 1942/43, 1943/44, 1944/45, 1947/48, 1949/50, 1953/54, 1956/57
Glasgow Merchants' Charity Cup: 1942, 1944, 1945, 1946, 1947, 1948, 1951
Player of the Year: 1955

— LET THERE BE LIGHT —

On 4th November 1878 Rangers played their first ever game under artificial light, floodlight as we would call it today. The venue was First Hampden, the opposition the Third Lanark Rifle Volunteers. Thirds won 3–2 before 6,000 spectators and the experiment was by no means a failure, although Saturday afternoon was still regarded as the regular time to play football.

— RANGERS MANAGERS: SCOT SYMON (1954–67) —

Born in Errol, Perthshire in 1911, James Scotland (Scot) Symon had a distinguished playing career with Dundee, Portsmouth and Rangers before embarking on a managerial career of some note with both East Fife and Preston North End. During Symon's playing career he achieved the rare distinction of playing for Scotland at both football and cricket.

He succeeded Bill Struth as Rangers manager in 1954 and in 13 years in charge he led the club to 15 trophy successes as well as two European finals. Indeed, he was the first Ibrox boss to experience European competition. He was one of the last of the Homburg managers – not one for the tracksuit and the training ground. Perhaps his biggest achievement was in building the great Rangers team of the early 1960s, the team of Jim Baxter, Ian McMillan, Jimmy Millar and Ralph Brand, the team that won the Triple Crown in 1963/64. He was in many ways a private, almost introverted, man and was never at ease with the media. He left Rangers in 1967, the manner of his parting lacking dignity.

Scot Symon's honours
League championship: 1955/56, 1956/57, 1958/59, 1960/61, 1962/63, 1963/64
Scottish Cup: 1960, 1962, 1963, 1964, 1966
Scottish League Cup: 1960/61, 1961/62, 1963/64, 1964/65

— LEAGUE TITLE WORLD RECORD —

Rangers' total of 52 domestic league titles is a record unmatched by any other club in the world. As of the start of the 2009/10 season, the clubs with the most titles are:

Club	Country	League titles
Rangers	Scotland	52
Linfield	Northern Ireland	48
Penarol	Uruguay	47
Celtic	Scotland	42
Nacional	Uruguay	41

— RANGERS LEGENDS: JIM BAXTER (1960–65; 1969–70) —

The superbly gifted Jim Baxter

An absolute genius with the ball at his feet, Jim Baxter was a superbly gifted player whose time at Rangers was alas all too short.

Baxter was the finest talent of a truly great Rangers team, that of the early 1960s. Indeed, in the estimation of many shrewd judges he was the finest Scottish talent of the past 60 years, and certainly Rangers' best left-sided player since Alan Morton. An extravagantly gifted, world-class wing half, 'Slim Jim' controlled the midfield with a magical left foot that could slice open the tightest defence.

The bigger the stage, the better . . . Celtic, Europe, international matches against England – Baxter was in his element in these titanic clashes. He had the arrogance and supreme confidence of a master – and, at times, would toy with opponents in a way which might lead to charges of showboating today. The 1963 Scottish Cup Final replay against Celtic was a case in point. Rangers led 3–0 midway through the second half and could have piled on more goals but Baxter preferred simply to deprive the opposition of the ball. Similarly at Wembley in 1967 he played keepie uppie against the world champions England in the closing stages of Scotland's 3–2 victory. As Jim later recalled, "We settled for extracting the urine . . ." Four years earlier, in 1963, the Empire Stadium was host to another of Baxter's Wembley displays as he scored both goals in a 2–1 victory for a Scotland side reduced to ten men as early as the sixth minute (in the days before substitutes) through captain Eric Caldow's broken leg. In the same year, he played for the Rest of the World against England in a game to mark the Football Association's centenary.

Europe was a stage the iconic 'Stanley' relished. In the Ibrox rain he tore West German side Borussia Mönchengladbach apart in November 1960 – Rangers winning 8–0. Among the crowd was Alex Ferguson, who would later rate Baxter's display that night as the finest he had ever witnessed. The following year in Monaco, Baxter put on masterclass in front of Prince Rainier and Princess Grace as Rangers won 3–2. Another superb performance away to Rapid Vienna in 1964 helped Rangers to progress to the quarter-finals of the European Cup, before his leg was broken by a late tackle in the dying minutes.

Baxter left Ibrox in June 1965, a wages dispute that had rumbled on for years eventually leading to his transfer to Sunderland for a £72,500 fee. He returned to Rangers in 1969, but by then an extravagant lifestyle had taken its toll and there were only occasional flashes of the old Baxter brilliance.

The arrival of Willie Waddell as manager in December 1969 spelled the end for Baxter, who was perhaps just too much of a loose cannon for the disciplinarian boss, and he retired in June 1970 aged just 30. In some respects his career had self-destructed, his problems being mirrored by those of George Best south of the border.

Baxter died in April 2001 after a brief battle with cancer at the all-too-young age of 61, his death being mourned by all of

Scotland. His funeral service, held in Glasgow Cathedral, was akin to a state occasion with the then Chancellor of the Exchequer Gordon Brown, Lord MacFarlane of Bearsden and Glasgow's Lord Provost Alex Mosson among those paying their final respects.

Jim Baxter factfile
Born: Hill of Beath, Fife, 29th September 1939
Died: 14th April 2001
Appearances: 254
Goals: 24
Full international appearances while at Rangers: 34 caps for Scotland
Honours:
League championship: 1960/61, 1962/63, 1963/64
Scottish FA Cup: 1962, 1963, 1964
Scottish League Cup: 1960/61, 1961/62, 1963/64, 1964/65

— GREAT EUROPEAN NIGHTS AT IBROX 5 —

Rangers 1   Inter Milan 0
Forrest

1964/64 European Cup, quarter-final, second leg
3rd March 1965
Attendance: 77,206

The defeat of both Red Star Belgrade and Rapid Vienna in the 1964/65 European Cup led many Rangers fans to believe that their team could become the first British club to lift Europe's premier competition. However, these dreams suffered a massive blow when the iconic Jim Baxter broke a leg in the closing minutes of a superb 2–0 win over Rapid in Vienna.

The draw for the last eight paired the Light Blues with world champions Inter Milan. Led by the formidable presence of coach Helenio Herrera, Inter's team included such world-class competitors as attacking full back Giacinto Facchetti, gifted inside forward Sandro Mazzola and winger Mario Corso. Together with Luis Suarez, midfield general and club captain, these were players of the highest calibre. Suarez in particular was Herrera's lieutenant on the field of play, the very fulcrum around which Inter's system revolved – he would be desperately missed when absent through injury in the 1967 Lisbon final.

The defending champions underlined their desire to retain the trophy with a 3–1 home win in the first leg, Rangers' first ever visit to the San Siro. Such a deficit, whilst not insurmountable, was certainly formidable against the masters of the art of 'catenaccio' (or bolt system). Rangers, however, got off to a stunning start in the Ibrox return two weeks later on a bitterly cold night when visiting goalkeeper Giuliano Sarti allowed a Roger Hynd drive to rebound off his chest into the path of Jim Forrest, who converted the rebound from close range.

The Italians demonstrated their experience however by shutting up shop after that early shock. Sweeper Picchi, in particular, was outstanding in central defence while the Light Blues were ineffective on the flanks where the threat of Willie Henderson was negated by Facchetti.

Rangers seldom looked like levelling the aggregate score until the 84th minute when George McLean's 18-yard shot from a Henderson cross slammed back off the crossbar with Sarti helpless. A 2–0 win would have meant a third match in Brussels, but time ran out on the Scottish champions and they were left to regret the absence of Baxter. Even without the great man, though, they had come within inches of taking the world champions to a third game.

To no one's surprise, Inter went on to retain the trophy when they defeated Benfica 1–0 in a final controversially staged in their very own Stadio San Siro. Two years later Glasgow's second club defeated an ageing Inter side missing four of their most important players, including their captain Luis Suarez, in the final in Lisbon.

Rangers team: Ritchie; Provan, Caldow; Greig, McKinnon, Hynd; Henderson, Millar, Forrest, McLean, Johnston

— OLDEST FA CUP WINNER —

When in 2009 David Weir captained Rangers to a 1–0 win over Falkirk in the Scottish FA Cup final he became the oldest player to have won a Scottish Cup winner's medal with Rangers. Born 10th May 1970, Weir was aged 39 years and 20 days when he won his third medal – having been a member of the successful Hearts team in 1998 as well as the Rangers side of 2008.

Prior to 2008, the Ibrox record was held as follows:

Andy Cunningham (1928) 37 years, 2 months, 15 days

Jock Shaw (1950) 37 years, 4 months, 24 days

The oldest known cup winner with any club was Jimmy McMenemy (Partick Thistle 1921) at 40 years, 7 months, 23 days. However it is very difficult to be absolutely certain about this as registration of births only became a statutory legal requirement in Scotland in 1857 which causes problems in finding out about the early cup winners. For example Charles Campbell of Queen's Park won eight winner's medals, but his date of birth is unknown.

— CLUB NICKNAMES —

It is a common assumption that Rangers' nickname of the Light Blues refers to the club colours – but in fact originally the term was a reference to the youthfulness and lightness of build of the Rangers players compared to the older and more physical nature of many of their opponents. In particular press coverage of the 1877 Scottish Cup Final against Vale of Leven and the then Kinning Park outfit's training methods of being "out on the Queen's highway" early in the morning caught the public's imagination. The players were referred to in the press as the 'Light and speedy Blues', and thereafter Rangers became known as the Light Blues for short, although clearly this nickname through common usage was accepted as referring to the club's colours.

Another popular nickname used through many years is the Teddy Bears. The only logical explanation for this one, that has survived for at least 50 years, is that of *Bears* rhyming to an extent with *'Gers*. Similarly, for some time the Honey Pears was another popular nickname with the fans for much the same reason, although that would perhaps only be recalled by an older generation today. Although the nickname Light Blues remains the 'official' one, in many respects to the legion of fans the most popular one would be the Teddy Bears.

— RANGERS MANAGERS: DAVID WHITE (1967–69) —

David White's appointment as manager was criticised from the start. That he was too inexperienced and that he was not a former Rangers player were two common complaints. White was certainly lacking in experience – he had previously been Clyde manager before moving to Ibrox as assistant to Scot Symon, just five months before being catapulted into the hot seat following Symon's dismissal. He was the first Rangers manager who could genuinely be described as a tracksuit boss, and the first to socialise with his players.

He was, however, unfortunate in that his time coincided with the all-conquering era of Jock Stein at Celtic. Despite this the young manager came perilously close to breaking Stein's stranglehold. In his first season, 1967/68, the Light Blues went right to the final game of the league campaign undefeated only to concede a goal in the last minute of the last game (at home to Aberdeen) which denied them the title. Two years in charge yielded only a Glasgow Cup, and White became the first manager to fail to win a major trophy. His dismissal in November 1969 followed a calamitous European defeat at the hands of Górnik Zabrze.

David White's honours:
Glasgow Cup: 1968/69

— EARLY FINISH —

On 23rd April 1888 Rangers defeated Vale of Leven 5–3 at Second Hampden in a Glasgow Merchants' Charity Cup tie. No doubt to the surprise of the 3,000 spectators, the game was concluded ten minutes early in order that the Vale might catch the Alexandria train.

— RANGERS LEGENDS: JOHN GREIG (1960–78) —

John Greig: officially Rangers' greatest player

When John Greig was voted Greatest Ever Ranger by the fans in 1999, there were few dissenters. Greig had achieved legendary status during an 18-year career with Rangers. As captain, he led the club to the 1972 European Cup Winners' Cup triumph in Barcelona and also collected three league championships, four Scottish Cups and two League Cups.

In all he played 857 games for the club between 1960 and 1978 (second only to Dougie Gray), 755 of them competitive appearances. Uniquely, Greig played a part in three treble-winning Ibrox sides, two of them as captain. On two occasions, he captained Rangers in European finals – in the Cup Winners' Cup in Nuremberg in 1967 as well as Barcelona five years later (when barely fit).

The bare statistics tell only half the story, however. For a decade or more, Greig was the driving force behind the Light Blues whether playing at full back, in central defence or in midfield. For an all-too-brief period during the mid-1960s the halfback line of Greig, McKinnon and Baxter was surely amongst the finest in the club's history. Having been introduced to first-

RANGERS

Home and Away Kits

1872-2009

www.historicalkits.co.uk

1872-80

1880-83

1883-93

1893-1898

1898-99

1899-1904

1904-07

1907-09

1909-15

1911-12 (change)

1915-18

1918-19

1920-30

1920-21 (change)

1930-57

1921-23 (change)

1923-32 (change)

1933-37 (change)

1938-45 (change)

1949-50 (Cup change)

1950-60 (change)

1950-60 (change 2)

1951-52 (change)

1950-57 (change)

1957-68

1961-69 (change)

1968-73

1973-78

1978-82

1978-82 (change)

1982-84

1982-84 (change)

1984-87

1984-87 (change)

1987-90

1987-88 (change)

1990-92

1990-92 (change)

1992-94

1992-93 (change)

1993-95 (change)

1993-94 (third)

1994-96

1995-96 (change)

1996-97

1996-97 (change)

1996-97 (third)

1997-99

1997-98 (change)

1998-99 (change)

1999-2001

1999-2000 (change) 2000-01 (change) 2001-02

2001-02 (change) 2002-03 2002-03 (change)

2002-03 (third) 2003-05 2003-04 (change)

2004-05 (change) 2005-06 2005-06 (change)

2005-06 (third)

2006-07

2006-07 (change)

2007-08

2007-08 (change 1)

2007-08 (change 2)

2007-08 (third)

2008 (UEFA Cup Final)

2008-09

2008-09 (change)

2009-10

team action during the great years of the early 1960s, for years thereafter he carried the Ibrox men during the years of Celtic dominance, leading the team from those dark days to the success of the 1970s under managers Willie Waddell and Jock Wallace. Although his duties were primarily defensive, he notched 120 goals for the club – an impressive tally for a non-forward by any reckoning.

In 1978, a year after being awarded an MBE, he was granted a testimonial match by the club – the first Rangers player to be so honoured since David Meiklejohn half a century earlier. A remarkable crowd of 65,000 saw Rangers overwhelm a Scotland side bound for the Argentina World Cup 5–0, a foretaste of what awaited Ally McLeod's team in South America.

Greig made 44 international appearances for Scotland, the first of which was against the Auld Enemy at Hampden Park in 1964, the Scots winning 1–0. Perhaps his most famous moment in the international arena arrived at the same venue the following year when he scored a last-minute winner to defeat Italy 1–0 in a World Cup qualifier.

He moved directly from the dressing room to the manager's office, and whilst it is fair to say that his five years as boss were not the most successful in the club's history there were still two successes in the Scottish Cup and League Cup as well as several impressive wins in Europe over the likes of Juventus, PSV Eindhoven and Borussia Dortmund. Crucially, however, Greig failed to secure the league championship, and with the pressure mounting his resignation as manager in November 1983 was perhaps inevitable.

A career change took him into the travel industry and then broadcasting, but he returned to Ibrox as public relations officer in January 1990. When Dick Advocaat became Rangers manager in the summer of 1998 he recognised a kindred spirit in Greig, whose career completed a full circle as he joined the Little General's coaching staff.

Early in 2004 John Greig was appointed a Director of Rangers Football Club, thus following in the footsteps of former managers Bill Struth, Willie Waddell, Graeme Souness and Walter Smith who had all served on the board.

John Greig factfile
Born: Edinburgh, 11th September 1942
Appearances: 755
Goals: 120
Full international appearances while at Rangers: 44 caps for Scotland
Honours:
European Cup Winners' Cup: 1972
League championship: 1962/63, 1963/64, 1974/75, 1975/76, 1977/78
Scottish FA Cup: 1963, 1964, 1966, 1973, 1976, 1978
Scottish League Cup: 1963/64, 1964/65, 1975/76, 1977/78
Player of the Year: 1966, 1976

— THE MATCH THAT COUNTED TWICE —

On 6th May 1905 Rangers lost 2–1 to Celtic at Hampden Park in a game that doubled as both the 1904/05 league championship play-off and as Rangers' home Glasgow League fixture.

THREE MEN SHORT —

During the First World War clubs faced great difficulties in fulfilling fixtures, even if restrictions on professional football were not as severe as they would be in the Second World War. Rangers were particularly badly affected at Falkirk on 20th November 1915. Already short-handed because of injury, illness and government work, Rangers arrived three players short after Andy Cunningham, Joe Hendry, and goalkeeper John Hempsey missed their rail connection in Glasgow due to fog. With veteran inside forward Alex Bennett, who had not played at all that season, being drafted in to play in goal, Rangers started the match with just nine men. To make matters worse, if that were possible, winger Scott Duncan (a future Manchester United manager) was injured in the first half and consequently missed the entire second period of play, leaving the Ibrox men with just eight players. Unsurprisingly, Falkirk won 2–0!

— GREAT EUROPEAN NIGHTS AT IBROX 6 —

Rangers 2   Real Zaragoza 0
D Smith
Willoughby

European Cup Winners' Cup, quarter-final, first leg
1st March 1967
Attendance: 65,000

It was back to the Cup Winners' Cup in season 1966/67 following Rangers' 1–0 triumph over Celtic in the 1966 Scottish FA Cup Final replay courtesy of a memorable Kai Johansen goal. Victories over Glentoran and holders Borussia Dortmund in the opening two rounds took the Ibrox men to the last eight of a European competition once again. The triumph over Dortmund was an outstanding result – the West Germans had won the trophy at Hampden Park the previous season, defeating Bill Shankly's Liverpool 2–1 after extra time.

Following Rangers' magnificent triumph they faced opponents whom John Greig later rated as the finest team encountered that season – Real Zaragoza of Spain, who had already proved their worth by eliminating Everton in the previous round and who clearly enjoyed confronting British opposition. *En route* to the Inter Cities Fairs Cup Final of 1965/66 (where they lost to Barcelona) Zaragoza had eliminated Hearts, Dunfermline Athletic and Leeds United! Rangers were desperate for cup success, having already been eliminated from the Scottish Cup by minnows Berwick Rangers.

Ibrox was bathed in a new Philips floodlighting system on the night, ironically an identical one to that which lit up the Rock of Gibraltar! As if that were not enough of an omen, the heavens opened to greet Zaragoza with rain, snow and sleet. Rangers revelled in the atrocious conditions, playing a standard of football which threatened to swamp the Spanish.

After ten minutes Dave Smith opened the scoring from a chance created by his namesake Alex, and when Alex Willoughby notched a second in 27 minutes the Spaniards were reeling.

Midway through the second half Dave Smith again found the net with a free kick only for Dutch referee Lauren van Ravens to order that the kick be retaken. So, Rangers had to be content with a 2–0 lead for the second leg, a result which they would certainly have accepted before the start.

In a dramatic return at La Romareda Rangers went through on the toss of a coin, and would go on to become the first British club to reach a second European final, going down 1–0 to Bayern Munich in their own backyard of Nuremberg.

Rangers team: Martin; Johansen, Provan; Jardine, McKinnon, Greig; Henderson, Willoughby, A Smith, D Smith, Wilson

— RANGERS MANAGERS: WILLIE WADDELL
(1969–72) —

In the long history of Rangers Football Club no single person has surely made a greater contribution than Willie Waddell as player, manager, general manager, managing director and vice-chairman.

His playing career was long and distinguished – as a winger of power and pace he thrilled the Ibrox crowds from 1938 to 1956, forming a devastating attacking combination with lifelong friend and colleague Willie Thornton. Waddell was a successful manager of Kilmarnock from 1957 to 1965, remarkably leading them to the league championship in 1964/65 – the last truly provincial club to achieve this. He was a successful sports journalist for the next four years before returning to Ibrox as manager where he ended a four-year trophy drought and led the club to their first (and to date only) European trophy in 1972. He worked tirelessly on behalf of the club following the 1971 Ibrox Disaster and as a director he oversaw the rebuilding of the stadium from 1978 to 1981. His name lives on in the Waddell Suite at Ibrox.

Willie Waddell's honours:
European Cup Winners' Cup: 1972
Scottish League Cup: 1970/71

— EUROPEAN FINALS: CUP WINNERS' CUP, 1967 —

Rangers qualified for their second European final in seven years – the 1966/67 European Cup Winners' Cup – eliminating Glentoran, Borussia Dortmund, Real Zaragoza and Slavia Sofia *en route*. Their opponents in the final were Bayern Munich, who had the advantage of playing in Nuremberg, just over 100 miles from Munich. Perhaps predictably, the handicap of playing in Bayern's own backyard would prove too great – with Rangers dreams of success bunkered in the Reichsparteitaggelande.

Bayern were a young, emerging side. Incredibly, they were excluded from the first national league championship (Bundesliga) when it was formed in 1963/64. Not considered either good enough or a big enough club, they would remain in the 'Regionalliga Sud' for just one more season before gaining promotion and proceeding to take the Bundesliga by storm, finishing a remarkable third in their first season and claiming the DFB Cup for a second time with a 4–3 win over Meiderich in Frankfurt – a success that was a passport to the European Cup Winners' Cup where, *en route* to the final, they eliminated Tartan Presov, Shamrock Rovers, Rapid Vienna and Standard Liège.

Bayern's emergence had been built around a young group of players, all in their early 20s, who would develop into world-class players over the next decade – specifically goalkeeper Sepp Maier, libero/midfield playmaker Franz Beckenbauer (already well known in Britain after starring in the 1966 World Cup), midfielder Franz Roth and a goalscorer who would go on to create all manner of records during his playing career, Gerd Müller.

Some 7,500 Rangers fans travelled to Nuremberg for the game – there would undoubtedly have been considerably more had the tickets been forthcoming, but the presence of a German team in the final had restricted availability somewhat.

Rangers were under considerable pressure prior to kick-off, having won no silverware thus far that season. Team selection for Nuremberg demonstrated the idiosyncratic management style of Scot Symon. Goalscorers had been jettisoned like confetti that season, with Jim Forrest and George McLean both discarded following the catastrophic Scottish Cup exit at the hands of

Berwick Rangers, and Alex Willoughby dropped, to accommodate defender Roger Hynd in attack, despite scoring 16 goals in 13 games in the second half of the season. Forrest's goalscoring record was exceptional – 145 goals in 163 competitive games for the club, including six in the European Cup campaign of 1964/65. The self-imposed exile of all three forwards would cost the Ibrox club dear.

Rangers based themselves in Neundettelsau, some 20 miles outside of Nuremberg – a mistake as it turned out for the lack of atmosphere and distance from the city meant that the party lost the big-match feel of the occasion.

The final itself was a dour struggle with defences well on top. A Hynd goal was disallowed for offside, and the centre forward also missed a golden opportunity from a Dave Smith pass in 33 minutes, his weak shot producing a fine one-handed save from Maier. An honest, wholehearted player lamentably lacking in pace and skill, Hynd was no match for the class of the young Beckenbauer. Rangers' wingers Henderson and Johnston were marked out of the game by the Bayern full backs.

The winner, deep into extra time, came from Franz Roth with a spectacular hook shot in 109 minutes from a long through ball from Beckenbauer. The very same Roth, nine years later, would net the only goal of the game in the European Cup Final at Hampden against St Etienne.

Defeat for Rangers was devastating. Manager Scot Symon never said a word after the game, locking himself in his hotel room without acknowledging a single person. Six months later, his 13-year reign as Ibrox boss would end. Chairman John Lawrence would in years to come lament Roger Hynd's miss, suggesting that it had cost him a knighthood.

European Cup Winners' Cup Final
Wednesday 31st May 1967
Nürnbergerstadion, Nuremberg
Bayern Munich 1 (Roth) Rangers 0
Attendance: 69,500

Rangers team: Martin; Johansen, Provan; Jardine, McKinnon, Greig; Henderson, A Smith, Hynd, D Smith, Johnston

— RANGERS LEGENDS: SANDY JARDINE (1965–82) —

Sandy Jardine: 17 years as a Ranger

A full back of the highest class, Sandy Jardine made his debut for Rangers under Scot Symon at the age of just 18 in the wake of the disastrous loss to Berwick Rangers in the 1967 Scottish FA Cup. Originally a wing half, he was utilised as a withdrawn centre forward by David White, then converted into a full back by Willie Waddell. In all, he played under five Rangers managers (Jock Wallace and John Greig being the others), one of the few players in the club's history to so do.

Christened William Pullar Jardine, the nickname 'Sandy' was given to him by the then Ibrox trainer/physiotherapist Davie Kinnear as Jardine's running motion reminded him of someone running through sand.

A cultured, elegant footballer, Jardine was one of the finest to play for the club in the entire post-war period. He played in two European finals for Rangers – in 1967 the young Sandy was praised by Bayern Munich's Franz Beckenbauer for his performance in Nuremberg, and five years later he was a key member of the Rangers team that triumphed in Barcelona.

An attacking full back of some pace who honed his speed at

the Powderhall Sprints, Jardine was a goalscorer as well – and some of his strikes were memorable ones. These included a thundering 20-yard drive in a league game against Celtic in May 1967, a superb run and chip over the goalkeeper in a League Cup tie at Motherwell in August 1975, and a scintillating solo run of some 75 yards in length, switching the ball from right foot to left before curling a 20-yarder into the top corner of the net in the Drybrough Cup Final of 1979.

The first three years of Sandy Jardine's first-team career at Ibrox were not successful ones as the club trailed in the shadow of Jock Stein's Celtic – but the full back soon made amends with 14 winners' medals in the next 12 years.

Under manager John Greig he was employed as a sweeper in European away games and selected domestic fixtures to considerable success, underlining the versatility of an outstanding club servant.

Thirty-eight international appearances were scant reward for a player of Jardine's class. Many shrewd observers believed that he was overlooked in favour of inferior players by Scotland boss Ally McLeod in particular. Nevertheless, he played in two World Cups, the only Rangers player ever to achieve such a mark whilst with the club. He was twice voted 'Player of the Year' (in 1975 and 1986), one of the few to have been so honoured.

Following 17 years as a Ranger Sandy was released after playing in the 1982 Scottish Cup Final. Many believed that this was a premature move – and so it proved, for he would enjoy an Indian summer with Hearts, coming agonisingly close to the league and cup double in 1985/86. He was appointed assistant manager at Tynecastle, then subsequently joint manager with former Ibrox colleague Alex MacDonald before leaving Hearts in 1988. He moved into the business world, then returned to Ibrox with the club's commercial department.

Sandy Jardine factfile
Born: Edinburgh, 31st December 1948
Appearances: 674
Goals: 77
Full international appearances while at Rangers: 38 caps for Scotland

Honours:
European Cup Winners' Cup 1972
League championship: 1974/75, 1975/76, 1977/78
Scottish FA Cup: 1973, 1976, 1978, 1979, 1981
Scottish League Cup: 1970/71, 1975/76, 1977/78, 1978/79, 1981/82
Player of the Year: 1975, 1986

— THE 1971 IBROX DISASTER —

Sixty-nine years after the First Ibrox Disaster tragedy once again enshrouded the stadium on 2nd January 1971 when 66 fans died at the end of the traditional New Year derby with Celtic. Even more so than in 1902, the disaster would have far-reaching consequences in terms of both ground safety and design.

On a cold winter's day a capacity 85,000 audience had watched as an enthralling game appeared to be heading for a goalless draw. In the 89th minute, though, a Bobby Lennox 20-yard shot struck the crossbar, the rebound being headed into the net by Jimmy Johnstone. Celtic appeared set for their first Ibrox win at New Year for fully half a century, yet in the next instant Dave Smith's free kick from the left was miskicked by Derek Johnstone but fell perfectly for Colin Stein to rifle the ball home.

The final whistle signalled a 1–1 draw, and the spectators headed for the exits, the Rangers fans in exuberant mood. The most popular exit from the ground was Stairway 13, located in the north-east corner at the Copland Road End, where perhaps as much as 25 per cent of the crowd poured down the wide, sweeping passageways towards Copland Road and the subway.

The stairways, built at three corners of the stadium, were 30 feet wide with steel railings and rigid wooden walls held secure by embedded railway sleepers, reinforced by concrete. Perhaps significantly, Stairway 13 was the steepest of the three.

As the buoyant 'Gers fans poured out someone in the crowd stumbled and fell, or perhaps bent down to pick up a fallen scarf, and such was the downward pressure from the packed ranks of those following behind that no one could stop to render assistance as, to quote one eye-witness report, "the crowd just caved in, like a pack of cards, as if all of them were falling into a huge hole." Those following behind, unaware of what had happened below them, pushed from the top of the stairway creating an intolerable pressure. People were crushed to death, many of them within seconds, many still standing upright. The death toll was 66, with a further 145 injured.

The central steel barriers that ran the length of the stairway were buckled and twisted. The outer wooden barriers had been so strongly built, so high and rigid, that they did not break, many of the fatalities being crushed against them.

The Fatal Accident Enquiry clearly established the time of the tragedy as being more than five minutes after the final whistle, thus giving the lie to the theory, which had absolutely no basis in fact, that Stein's late goal had been a contributory factor in causing departing fans to turn back and return up the stairs to the terracing. The simple truth was that it was utterly impossible to turn against the flow of the crowd on a packed stairway.

There had been prior warnings with three accidents in the previous ten years, all on the same stairway. In 1961 two people had died and 44 injured in what to many people is the forgotten Ibrox Disaster. Changes made following that tragedy, presumably on the expert advice of the day, actually contributed to the cataclysmic events of a decade later. Eleven people were injured in 1967, 30 in 1969 – but sadly it is for 2nd January 1971 that Stairway 13 will always be remembered.

As in 1902, the vast majority of the Ibrox audience (including the author of this book) had gone home completely unaware of the disaster, and as with that previous tragedy the effects would be far-reaching in terms of stadium design.

Rangers manager Willie Waddell worked tirelessly to ensure that the club was represented at every funeral, that the injured were visited and that the problems of Stairway 13 were addressed immediately. Waddell saw that the way ahead was for the vast sweeping terracing of the oval bowl to be swept away, that the days of 100,000 crowds standing in the rain on open terracing were gone, all long before Bradford, Hillsborough and the Taylor Report. He studied stadium design in Germany, Italy and elsewhere and for the next ten years, as manager, general manager and managing director, would be the driving force in creating the magnificent, modern stadium of today – the finest in Scotland and one of Europe's best.

— SECOND WORLD WAR HEROES —

The following Rangers players saw active service in the British Army during the Second World War: David Kinnear, Tom McKillop, James Galloway, Willie Thornton (trooper in the Scottish Horse Regiment), Eddie Rutherford, Alistair McKillop, David Marshall, Willie Paton, Jimmy Parlane, Donald McLatchie (gunner in the Royal Artillery), Thomas Souter (captain in the Royal Scots Fusiliers), Sammy Cox (Gordon Highlanders), David Gray (served in the Middle East), Archie Macauley (Army Physical Training Corps), Dr Adam Little (Royal Medical Corps), Joe Johnston, Willie Knox, R Cowan, P Grant, A Beattie, GDF Mackay.

Chris McNee (flight lieutenant), Ian McPherson, Eddie Rutherford, Jimmy Simpson and Alex Stevenson all served in the Royal Air Force, while Jimmy Parlane, Billy Williamson and Bobby Brown (Petty Officer – Fleet Air Arm) served in the Royal Navy.

Willie Thornton was awarded the Military Medal following action in Sicily and Ian McPherson, who flew on the first RAF bombing raid on Germany, received the Distinguished Flying Cross.

Former Rangers player Carl Hansen was arrested in his native Copenhagen in 1943. A member of the Danish resistance, he was sentenced to four months imprisonment by the Nazi Occupation forces.

— CRUCIAL CORNER COUNT —

Rangers won the 1942/43 Southern League, a wartime forerunner of the Scottish League Cup, 11–3 on corners against Falkirk after a 1–1 draw at Hampden Park. The following year Rangers were held to a 0–0 draw in the final by Hibs, but this time lost out 6–5 on corner kicks.

— RANGERS MANAGERS: JOCK WALLACE (1972–78; 1983–86) —

Jock Wallace will go down in history as the man who broke Jock Stein's domination of Scottish football, leading the club to the league championship in 1974/75 after a barren 11-year period.

Wallace had enjoyed a varied playing career as a goalkeeper whilst seeing active service in Malaysia with the King's Own Scottish Borderers, but it was as player-manager of Berwick Rangers that he truly made his mark when he kept a clean sheet in the Shielfield club's sensational 1–0 Scottish Cup win in 1967. A lifelong bluenose, he joined Rangers as coach in 1970, playing a key role in the 1971/72 European campaign that ended in triumph in Barcelona, and succeeded to the manager's chair that summer. He was a supreme motivator, and is the only Rangers manager to date to win two trebles, yet he rocked the club to its foundations with his shock resignation in the summer of 1978. He returned to Ibrox five years later and immediately resurrected an ailing club to secure the League Cup within four months. Ill health denied Jock the opportunity to build on that success, and he left Rangers in April 1986. Nevertheless, there are those who, to this day, would rate Jock Wallace as the greatest Rangers manager of them all.

Jock Wallace's honours:
League championship: 1974/75, 1975/76, 1977/78
Scottish Cup: 1973, 1976, 1978
Scottish League Cup: 1975/76, 1977/78, 1983/84, 1984/85

— GREAT EUROPEAN NIGHTS AT IBROX 7 —

Rangers 1	Górnik Zabrze 3
Baxter	Olek
	Lubanski
	Skowroknok

1969/70 European Cup Winners' Cup, second round, second leg
26th November 1969
Attendance: 70,000

Having overcome Steaua Bucharest in the opening round of the 1969/70 Cup Winners' Cup, Rangers found themselves returning to Eastern Europe for a second successive occasion. On a first ever visit to Poland, Rangers had the daunting prospect of facing Górnik Zabrze, a side that Sir Matt Busby had rated as the best Manchester United had met *en route* to their European Cup success a year earlier.

Tactical naivety cost the visitors dear in the first leg in Chorzow, Górnik winning 3–1. Such a deficit was by no means an insurmountable one for the Ibrox return, yet the job in hand was scarcely helped when, with the team based at Largs, both Jim Baxter and Willie Henderson missed training on the day before the game, having overslept. Manager David White chose to field both players regardless, a decision that drew criticism from many Ibrox traditionalists.

The game started well for the Light Blues, when Baxter opened the scoring after 18 minutes and had Willie Johnston not shot wide from six yards early in the second half then the story of the night might well have been wholly different. Instead, a lightning break ended with Alfred Olek netting the equaliser from a narrow angle with Gerry Neef at fault.

Rangers were right up against it and a superb individual goal from Włodzimierz Lubanski after 77 minutes effectively ended their interest in the competition. Collecting the ball on the halfway line, he left McKinnon trailing as he advanced towards the penalty area only to be forced wide by Neef. Virtually on the goal-line, Lubanski turned back as if to head towards his own goal only to wrong-foot two defenders as he swiftly changed direction, turning sharply to rifle the ball into the roof of the net from a tight angle. It was a strike worthy of winning any game, as was appreciated by the Ibrox legions, who sportingly applauded a class player and team.

Five minutes later Skowroknok added a third with Neef found wanting again as the Pole advanced through the middle before curling the ball home from 20 yards.

The superb Górnik side received a warm ovation from the 70,000 crowd as they left the field at the end of the game. The Poles would go all the way to the final that season before losing, most unluckily, to Manchester City in Vienna in a game played in appalling weather conditions that undoubtedly influenced the outcome.

Rangers' defeat led to demonstrations in Edmiston Drive demanding the head of David White. The criticism was to an extent justified. Most crucially, White had failed to break the iron grip exerted on Scottish football by Jock Stein's Celtic. With specific regard to the Górnik game, he had not taken the trouble to watch the opposition beforehand, he was tactically inept in Chorzow, and he was demonstrably lacking in authority and discipline when failing to take action against 'the Largs Two'.

As it turned out, the defeat had major repercussions for the club. David White was sacked the very next morning, to be replaced by Willie Waddell. Had a coin fallen on the other side in Lisbon that same evening, thus eliminating Celtic instead of Benfica, the Ibrox manager may well have survived.

Rangers team: Neef; Johansen, Heron; Greig, McKinnon, Baxter; Henderson, Penman, Stein, Johnston, Persson (A MacDonald)

— TAKING ON THE ENGLISH —

Rangers' results against English teams in the FA Cup and European competitions:

Date	Competition	Result
30th Oct 1886	FA Cup	Everton 0 Rangers 1
21st Nov 1886	FA Cup	Rangers 2 Church 1
29th Jan 1887	FA Cup	Rangers 3 Lincoln City 0
19th Feb 1887	FA Cup	Rangers 5 Old Westminsters 1
5th March 1887	FA Cup	Aston Villa 3 Rangers 1
29th March 1961	Cup Winners' Cup	Rangers 2 Wolves 0
19th April 1961	Cup Winners' Cup	Wolves 1 Rangers 1
31st Oct 1962	Cup Winners' Cup	Spurs 5 Rangers 2
11th Dec 1962	Cup Winners' Cup	Rangers 2 Spurs 3
26th March 1968	Fairs Cup	Rangers 0 Leeds 0

9th April 1968	Fairs Cup	Leeds 2 Rangers 0
14th May 1969	Fairs Cup	Rangers 0 Newcastle 0
21st May 1969	Fairs Cup	Newcastle 2 Rangers 0
21st Oct 1992	European Cup	Rangers 2 Leeds 1
11th Nov 1992	European Cup	Leeds 1 Rangers 2
22nd Oct 2003	Champions League	Rangers 0 Man Utd 1
4th Nov 2003	Champions League	Man Utd 3 Rangers 0

— NINE-IN-A-ROW —

Between seasons 1988/89 and 1996/97 Rangers won an extraordinary nine league titles on the trot. Surprisingly, perhaps, Rangers' main challenger over this period was Aberdeen rather than Celtic. Here's how the top of the table looked at the end of those nine never-to-be-forgotten seasons:

Season	1st	2nd	3rd
1988/89	Rangers (56 pts)	Aberdeen (50 pts)	Celtic (46 pts)
1989/90	Rangers (51 pts)	Aberdeen (44 pts)	Hearts (44 pts)
1990/91	Rangers (55 pts)	Aberdeen (53 pts)	Celtic (41 pts)
1991/92	Rangers (72 pts)	Hearts (63 pts)	Celtic (62 pts)
1992/93	Rangers (73 pts)	Aberdeen (64 pts)	Celtic (60 pts)
1993/94	Rangers (58 pts)	Aberdeen (55 pts)	Motherwell (54 pts)
1994/95	Rangers (69 pts)	Motherwell (54 pts)	Hibs (53 pts)
1995/96	Rangers (87 pts)	Celtic (83 pts)	Aberdeen (55 pts)
1996/97	Rangers (80 pts)	Celtic (75 pts)	Dundee United (60 pts)

Rangers had a great chance to make it a record-breaking ten-in-a-row in 1997/98 but two defeats in their last four matches – away to Aberdeen and at home to Kilmarnock – opened the door for Celtic who won the league by just two points.

— SPLASHING THE CASH —

Rangers' record signing is lanky Norwegian striker Tore André Flo, who joined the club from Chelsea for £12.5 million in 2000. As the following list shows, Rangers' other big money signings have not even approached the fee paid for the Scandinavian targetman:

Fee	Year	Player	Signed from
£12.5m	2000	Tore André Flo	Chelsea
£6.5m	2001	Michael Ball	Everton
£6m	2002	Mikel Arteta	Barcelona
£5.5m	1998	Andrei Kanchelskis	Fiorentina
£5m	1998	Giovanni van Bronckhorst	Feyenoord

— FIXTURE CONFUSION —

On New Year's Day 1889 Rangers lost 6–2 at Blackburn Rovers in a 'Challenge Match' before 7,000 spectators. Meanwhile, back in Glasgow, a bemused Aston Villa team had turned up at First Ibrox expecting to play the Light Blues only to find their opponents were nowhere to be seen.

— GREAT EUROPEAN NIGHTS AT IBROX 8 —

Rangers 2   Bayern Munich 0
Jardine
Parlane

European Cup Winners' Cup, semi-final, second leg
19th April 1972
Attendance: 80,000

When Rangers reached their fifth European semi-final in 1972, having eliminated Rennes, Sporting Lisbon and Torino *en route*, they received no luck when the draw paired them for the third time in six years with Bundesliga giants Bayern Munich.

Bayern were now an even more formidable force than before.

Within two months of the meeting with Rangers they would form the nucleus of the West German national side that would win the European Championships and go on two years later to claim the World Cup. All the big names were there: Franz Beckenbauer (European Footballer of the Year), Gerd Müller ('der Bomber der Nation'), Sepp Maier, Uli Hoeness, Paul Breitner and George Schwarzenbeck. A truly world-class outfit, Bayern had already eliminated Liverpool earlier in the tournament and would go on to success in three consecutive European Cup finals from 1974 to 1976.

In the first leg played at Grünwalder Stadion, Rangers secured a magnificent 1–1 draw. However, the outcome of the tie was far from a formality, and that hard truth was underlined just four days before the Ibrox return when inspirational captain John Greig received a bad ankle injury in the Scottish Cup semi-final at Hampden against Hibernian. A virus also hit the club, undoubtedly affecting their performance in the 1–1 draw at Hampden, and it had not fully cleared as the Light Blues prepared at Largs for the visit of Bayern.

Youngster Derek Parlane replaced the injured Greig, and Rangers could not have got off to a better start, opening the scoring in 45 seconds when Willie Johnston's cross from the left was only partially cleared by Beckenbauer. Derek Johnstone passed the loose ball to Sandy Jardine whose 25-yard floated cross-cum-shot totally deceived Maier.

Ibrox was a cauldron of noise and four minutes later it was almost 2–0 when Stein's header smacked off the crossbar. The second goal was merely delayed, however, Parlane's 15-yard volley finding the net via the underside of the crossbar following a Johnston corner.

Rangers were running Bayern ragged, and might have doubled their lead by the interval. Early in the second half Peter McCloy produced a fine save when turning a Hoeness shot onto the post – but the West Germans were rattled and squabbling amongst themselves, a beaten team.

"Barcelona Here We Come" sang 80,000 Rangers' fans at the end of a victory which was sweet revenge in particular for Nuremberg. On what was a remarkable night in Glasgow 75,000 spectators at Celtic Park witnessed a goalless draw with Inter Milan in the European Cup semi-final, the Italians going through on penalties. Rangers had finally found light at the end of the long, dark tunnel they had found themselves in since 1967, and of course would achieve the 'Holy Grail' when they achieved European success in the Catalan capital, defeating Dynamo Moscow 3–2 in the final.

Rangers team: McCloy; Jardine, Mathieson; Parlane, Jackson, Smith; McLean, Johnstone, Stein, A McDonald, Johnston

— RANGERS MANAGERS: JOHN GREIG (1978–83) —

John Greig moved directly from dressing room to manager's office following Jock Wallace's shock resignation. His appointment was certainly a risk in that he lacked any managerial experience whatsoever, having just captained the club to its second treble in three years.

In his first year in charge Greig's Rangers came agonisingly close to a dream campaign, winning both the League Cup and the Scottish FA Cup and attaining magnificent European Cup triumphs over Juventus and PSV Eindhoven only for a serious injury crisis to prove too great a handicap in the quarter-finals against Köln. The league championship should by any reckoning have been Ibrox-bound, only for a severe winter to lead to fixture congestion on top of the aforementioned injuries to deprive Rangers of the title. Sound familiar?

It was all downhill after that – an ageing squad and some dubious big-money signings meant that there was no serious championship challenge from Ibrox for the next four years despite two more trophy successes. The pressure finally told – and Greig resigned in November 1983. He returned to the club seven years later as public relations officer, and remains a director of the club to this day.

John Greig's honours
Scottish Cup: 1979, 1981
Scottish League Cup: 1978/79, 1981/82

— PACKING THEM IN —

Hampden Park was the venue for all the following matches, which attracted the biggest crowds ever to see Rangers in action:

Att.	Fixture	Result
143,570	1948 Scottish Cup semi-final	Rangers 1 Hibernian 0
133,750	1948 Scottish Cup Final replay	Rangers 1 Morton 0
132,870	1969 Scottish Cup Final	Rangers 0 Celtic 4
131,975	1948 Scottish Cup Final	Rangers 1 Morton 1
129,762	1953 Scottish Cup Final	Rangers 1 Aberdeen 1
129,643	1963 Scottish Cup Final	Rangers 1 Celtic 1
127,940	1962 Scottish Cup Final	Rangers 2 St Mirren 0
126,599	1966 Scottish Cup Final	Rangers 0 Celtic 0
125,154	1947 Scottish League Cup semi-final	Rangers 3 Hibernian 1
122,714	1973 Scottish Cup Final	Rangers 3 Celtic 2

— EUROPEAN FINALS: CUP WINNERS' CUP, 1972 —

The 1971/72 European campaign saw Rangers defeat Rennes, Sporting Lisbon, Torino and Bayern Munich on the way to the final. This was an exceptional standard of opposition with Bayern packed with international talent, Sporting and Torino league leaders in their respective countries. In the Barcelona final Rangers faced Dynamo Moscow who had previously eliminated Olympiakos Piraeus, Eskisehirspor of Turkey, Red Star Belgrade and Dynamo Berlin, with the last two home ties being staged in Tashkent and Lvov due to the severity of the Moscow winters.

There was a massive exodus of Light Blue followers to Barcelona with almost 25,000 travelling. Belief was widespread that after two European final defeats in 1961 and 1967 to Fiorentina and Bayern Munich respectively it would be a case of third time lucky.

Rangers, though, had injury worries. Captain John Greig played despite not having featured in a competitive match for six weeks, while centre half Colin Jackson was forced to withdraw after suffering an ankle injury in training.

The Nou Camp is one of the world's great arenas, and home to one of the world's great football clubs. In 1972 the stadium capacity stood at 100,000 – and even if the ground was only a quarter full it was still a colourful sight. Red, white and blue was everywhere – the Ibrox legions comprising at least 95 per cent of the 24,701 audience. Dynamo Moscow must have felt amongst the loneliest people in the world – none of their fans had been permitted to travel by the Soviet authorities, although this was a situation that their players must have been only too familiar with.

Dynamo midfield general and captain, the vastly experienced Josef Sabo, had been earmarked as the key to his team's play and was the subject of a hard, physical challenge from John Greig inside the opening five seconds. Greig had made the 'engine room' of the opposition aware of his presence, and would be a constant inspiration to his teammates as he drove them on to the 'Holy Grail' that Ibrox teams had striven for during the previous 16 years.

The Russians may not have been as glamorous a team as Rangers' semi-final opponents, but it did not take them long to demonstrate that they were every bit as dangerous – Yakubik shooting wide from a Baydachny cross on ten minutes. Seven minutes later Peter McCloy saved at the second attempt from a Makhovikov 30-yard shot.

Rangers had the bulk of the play and of possession, but there was a cutting edge to Dynamo that carried a definite threat. Nevertheless, the opening goal when it arrived in 24 minutes was for Rangers – a superb through-ball from Dave Smith releasing Colin Stein with the Dynamo defence hesitant. The Ibrox striker outpaced his marker Dolmatov and drove the ball unerringly home.

Rangers were now thrusting forward at every opportunity. Five minutes before the interval it was 2–0 when the skilful Dave Smith, Scotland's Footballer of the Year, moved forward effortlessly before wrong-footing the Russian defence with a quick turn and cross for Willie Johnston to head home.

The 'Gers left the field to a massive ovation at half-time, and quite unbelievably were three up four minutes after the restart when a long, high clearance from Peter McCloy found Johnston clear and unmarked in front of goal – the goalkeeper's sky-high kick-out having totally confused the Dynamo offside trap. 'Bud' executed his finish to perfection, and Rangers led by 3–0.

The game was not yet over, however – a misplaced pass by Willie Mathieson enabled Evryuzhikhin to feed the blatantly offside substitute Eshtrekov to net. Spanish referee Ortiz de Mendebel awarded the goal. Dynamo came more and more into the game as the second half wore on, and McCloy had to make an instinctive save to prevent a Sandy Jardine own goal. Frayed nerves were at boiling point on 87 minutes when Sasha Makhovikov scooped the ball home from a Gershkovich pass, thus ensuring a tense closing few minutes. As Dynamo poured forward one could almost smell an equalising goal.

Rangers' worries were scarcely helped when, in the final minute, the referee, in awarding a foul, gave a long blast on his whistle – cue for a mini pitch invasion from many 'Gers fans. When seconds later it was full time the 'Follow Follow' brigade poured on in their thousands to celebrate their club's great victory.

This was Rangers' finest hour – uniquely achieved in their centenary year. The Light Blues had defeated the cream of Europe *en route* to their greatest triumph – the standard of opposition being far superior than that encountered by the two British clubs that until 1972 had won the European Cup.

European Cup Winners' Cup Final
Wednesday 24th May 1972
Estadio Nou Camp, Barcelona
Attendance: 24,701
Rangers 3 (Johnston 2, Stein) Dynamo Moscow (Eshtrekov, Makhovikov)
Rangers team: McCloy; Jardine, Mathieson; Greig, Johnstone, Smith; McLean, Conn, Stein, A McDonald, Johnston

— THE RECORD: INTRODUCTION —

All sporting records are made to be broken, but for Rangers there is most certainly one record that can never be bettered, nor in all likelihood equalled. This is the club's ultimate one-season championship success of 1898/1899, a milestone that is untouchable, the ultimate embodiment of perfection.

Of all the outstanding achievements in the long and proud history of the Rangers Football Club, perhaps none can bear comparison with that campaign when not only was the league championship won for the first time in eight years, but it was won with a 100 per cent record – a statistic unmatched by any club anywhere in world football to this day.

In John Allan's *The Story of the Rangers*, an official but flawed history chronicling the club's first 50 years, the 100 per cent points haul the Govan team racked up in winning each of their 18 league fixtures is referred to simply as 'the Record'. "It stands in splendid isolation," the tome says of an accomplishment deemed "the greatest single achievement in the long Rangers story".

Unequalled anywhere in the world, before or since, it is unlikely to be challenged in more demanding times. The Ibrox club, though, had a far more modest aim than a clean sweep when embarking upon the 1898/99 season. Eight years on from sharing the inaugural league championship with Dumbarton, Rangers were still seeking their first outright title win. In the two previous years they had proved one-off specialists, lifting five of the six cups on offer, and there was no question that there were major talents in their ranks. A young set of players had grown up together into one of the great Rangers' teams.

Neilly Gibson has been described as the greatest wing half of Victorian times, indeed one of the greatest of all-time, while inside forward John McPherson was recognised as the finest player over the course of the club's first 50 years, not least because he played in every position, including goal. Others, such as their captain and prodigious centre forward, Robert Hamilton, who would bag 21 goals in the club's epoch-making campaign, and dependable defender Jock Drummond – the last player to wear a flat cap in senior games – made Rangers a formidable force. On the left wing, Alec Smith – a native of Darvel, Ayrshire – as indeed was Sammy Cox, another Ibrox legend half a century on. Along with Drummond, Nicol Smith formed what was possibly the finest full back partnership in the club's history.

Despite these talents there was concern that the squad was too lightweight to usurp their Old Firm rivals. Celtic were league top dogs, having themselves gone through the 1897/98 season unbeaten, winning 15 and drawing three of their matches. Only Nicol Smith, who died of enteric fever in 1905 while still a Rangers player, exceeded 12 stone. What Rangers lacked in bulk, however, they made up for with brio.

— BOYD'S BALLS —

Remarkably, the last five hat-tricks by a Rangers player have all been scored by Kris Boyd. Since signing from Kilmarnock in January 2006, Boyd has claimed the match ball in the following games:

Date	Competition	Result
7th Jan 2006	Scottish Cup 3rd	Rangers 5 Peterhead 0
2nd April 2006	Premier	Dundee United 1 Rangers 4
11th Feb 2007	Premier	Kilmarnock 1 Rangers 3
17th Mar 2007	Premier	Rangers 3 Aberdeen 0
23rd Jan 2008	Scottish Cup 4th	Rangers 6 East Stirling 0

— MADRID MASSACRE —

The day after Rangers were thrashed 6–0 by mighty Real Madrid in the first round of the European Cup in 1963 sportswriter Gair Henderson of the *Evening Times* fell into conversation with manager Scot Symon at Madrid Airport. Eager to spin a positive story, Symon offered the view that had Forrest converted a first-minute chance it would have been a very different matter. "Yes," replied Gair, "it would have been 6–1 . . ."

— THE RECORD: GAMES 1–11—

Rangers' record-breaking season began on 20th August 1898 in some style, when Partick Thistle were vanquished 6–2.

Injury threatened Rangers' progress at Tynecastle two weeks later. Nicol Smith, Jock Drummond and James Miller were all absent, obliging the Govan side to field a makeshift defence with McPherson at full back. The home side could count goalkeeper Harry Rennie and forward George Livingstone (both Rangers players in later years) amongst their ranks. The Glasgow side trailed to a 'Cocky' Taylor strike early in the game, but fought back with two goals from Hamilton and John Wilkie so that not even a late Livingstone penalty could deny them the points.

The sixth fixture took Rangers across the city to Celtic Park already holding a four-point advantage over their great rivals, and an attendance of 46,500 was testimony to the vital nature of the contest even this early in the season. Rangers' classical precision attacking football swept aside the power and physical strength of their great rivals. The outcome was the most decisive Rangers win at that venue, a sensational 4–0 triumph that left no dispute as to the superiority of the Light Blues, exacting perfect revenge for the identical scoreline of one year earlier, with goals from a Bobby Neil penalty, John McPherson, John Campbell and James Miller. Something had really started to stir.

Hearts were still championship contenders when they visited Ibrox on 1st October, underlined by the presence of a 25,000 audience. As at Tynecastle the Edinburgh side got off to a whirlwind start, taking the lead in ten minutes and looking like adding to their lead until in a swift counter-attack a solo run by Alec Smith created an opening for Hamilton to net. Two second-half goals from Hamilton again and Alec Smith secured a 3–1 win and effectively eliminated Hearts from the title race. At the halfway stage in the campaign Rangers led by three points from Hibernian.

The pivotal moment for the Record came in the 11th game at Hibernian on 19th November 1898. Edinburgh had not always been a happy hunting ground for the Blues. A match billed as a title decider, it looked as if Hibs were on their way when they opened up a 2–0 lead after 22 minutes. Rangers were up against it, but fought hard to retrieve the situation, levelling the game with goals on either side of half-time through Miller and Alec Smith. A fast and furious second half developed, with first Gemmell completing his hat-trick and Hamilton equalising. Rangers piled on the pressure, but a draw seemed a certain outcome until the 89th minute when John Campbell was fouled for a clear penalty that Neil coolly converted. It is recorded that he stepped back "as coolly as walking to church of Sunday to smite the ball into the net".

— RANGERS MANAGERS: DICK ADVOCAAT (1999–2001) —

Dutchman Dick Advocaat was the first foreigner to manage Rangers. 'The Little General' arrived at Ibrox with an outstanding CV, having won the Dutch league with PSV Eindhoven as well as leading the Netherlands to the last eight of the 1994 World Cup.

Advocaat enjoyed outstanding success in his first two seasons in Scotland, winning the treble in 1998/99 and the league and cup double one year later. He attracted quality players in abundance to Ibrox at a massive cost and achieved some outstanding results in Europe. He moved on in December 2001 to return to coaching his native Netherlands, leading them to the semi-finals of Euro 2004 in Portugal. Perhaps Advocaat's greatest achievement, however, was with Zenit Saint Petersburg, leading them to both the Russian league championship and, of course, the 2008 UEFA Cup.

Dick Advocaat's honours
League championship: 1998/99, 1999/2000
Scottish Cup: 1999, 2000
Scottish League Cup: 1998/99

— THE RECORD: GAMES 12–18 —

The record was still on. Rangers celebrated their near escape at Hibernian by overwhelming their next three opponents, scoring 20 goals for the loss of just two, although St Bernard also provided a scare on 3rd December, taking a 2–1 lead with just 15 minutes remaining. Only a "piece of individual paralysing brilliance" by John Campbell, in the form of a four-goal burst in ten minutes, brought Rangers a 5–2 win. The championship was duly sealed, courtesy of a 7–0 win over Dundee at Ibrox on 17th December with three goals from Hamilton and two apiece from Alec Smith and McPherson, leaving four matches to be navigated to achieve what had seemed impossible.

With the pursuit of perfection an increasing strain, there were fears over the first of these games, the return visit of Hibernian to Ibrox on Christmas Eve – potentially a difficult and explosive affair if a 100 per cent record was to be secured. Hibs had felt hard done by in Leith, yet were swept aside by a whirlwind home performance that netted five goals in the opening 20 minutes. Rangers went on to hit ten in total, Alec Smith netting four. The 10–0 scoreline represents a Rangers record-winning margin for a league game that stands to this day, and Hibs' worst league defeat, although ironically a late penalty miss by Campbell denied the club the opportunity to equal the Scottish league record of 11–0!

Celtic were first-footers – a real obstacle if ever there was one, but Rangers were in irresistible form before 30,000 spectators and again scored four goals, this time for the loss of just one, with Hamilton netting the first New Year hat-trick in the fixture.

The record attempt came down to the final game of the season, against Clyde at Shawfield in Arctic conditions on 7th January 1899. Rangers sealed the Record with a 3–0 win courtesy of goals from Alec Smith, Miller and a Neil penalty. Terrible conditions prevailed as Rangers determined to clinch the victory, and in truth there was never any doubt as to the final outcome.

Trailing in Rangers' wake, Hearts finished second, ten points adrift. The never-to-be forgotten feat proved an important landmark for the Ibrox club, who were champions for the next three years.

— RANGERS LEGENDS: ALLY MCCOIST (1983–98) —

Ally McCoist: icon of the modern era

'Super Ally' McCoist was Rangers' most iconic goalscorer of the modern era, with an incredible 355 goals in 581 appearances for the club.

He signed for Rangers at the third time of asking in June 1983 in a £175,000 transfer from Sunderland, having previously played for St Johnstone (for whom he scored his first goal at Ibrox in a Scottish Cup tie in February 1981). His first two years in Light Blue were difficult ones, but the young McCoist showed great strength of character (a trait admired by the then manager Jock Wallace) to work his way into the affection of the fans both by his penchant for scoring goals and through his effervescent, bubbling personality.

In an unforgettable Ibrox career Ally overcame the doubts of both the fans and of manager Graeme Souness to establish himself as the most popular Rangers player of his generation. He broke all manner of goalscoring records both at the club and in Scottish football and was a key member of the Nine-in-a-Row side.

He won a record nine League Cup winners' medals, scoring a club record 54 goals in the competition that included eight in finals. 'Super Ally' also found the net 27 times in Old Firm fixtures, a total bettered only by RC Hamilton who scored 36 goals against Celtic. In the European arena, 21 goals represented another club record. In both 1991/92 and 1992/93 he won the European Golden Boot with 34 league goals each year, despite suffering a broken leg in the second season which forced him to miss the last five games of the campaign.

Most impressively, perhaps, he set a new post-war Scottish league goalscoring record, surpassing the previous record holder Gordon Wallace in December 1996.

If McCoist will always be remembered for his goals, his longevity and durability should never be overlooked. He fought back from that broken leg, sustained in Portugal on international duty, and other injury problems to notch up a total of 418 league games for Rangers, a tally bettered only by five players in the club's history.

At international level, McCoist played in the 1990 World Cup Finals in Italy and at Euro 96 in England, scoring a memorable winning goal for Scotland against Switzerland at Villa Park.

Following Walter Smith's departure as Rangers manager in 1998, McCoist moved on to Kilmarnock where he played for three years, adding two more Scotland caps to the 59 he won while at Ibrox.

McCoist was a natural for television, and he wasted no time at the end of his playing career in carving a niche for himself on the popular BBC programme *A Question of Sport* as well as making regular appearances on ITV's UEFA Champions League coverage, before returning to Ibrox as assistant to Walter Smith in January 2007.

Ally McCoist factfile
Born: Bellshill, Lanarkshire, 24th September 1962
Appearances: 581
Goals: 355
Full international appearances while at Rangers: 59 caps for Scotland
Honours:
League championship: 1986/87, 1988/89, 1989/90, 1990/91, 1991/92, 1992/93, 1995/96, 1996/97
Scottish FA Cup: 1992
Scottish League Cup: 1983/84, 1984/85, 1986/87, 1987/88, 1988/89, 1990/91, 1992/93, 1993/94, 1996/97
Player of the Year: 1992
European Golden Boot: 1991/92, 1992/93

— RIVALS FROM THE MISTY PAST —

Rangers' record in all competitions against the seven fellow founder Scottish Football League members who later became defunct:

	P	W	D	L	F	A
Third Lanark (1872–1967)	144	98	27	19	359	158
Leith Athletic (1887–1954)*	15	13	1	1	47	17
Vale of Leven (1872–1929)**	13	4	5	4	27	19
Abercorn (1877–1920)	8	6	2	0	35	12
Renton (1872–1921)	7	5	1	1	23	14
Cambuslang (1874–97)	6	5	0	1	21	7
Cowlairs (1876–96)	4	3	1	0	14	3

*Reformed in 1996
**Reformed in 1939

— THE 1902 IBROX DISASTER IN VERSE —

A poignant reflection on the tragic events at Ibrox on 5th April
1902 is inscribed in these unattributed verses:

Lines on the Ibrox Disaster

Brightly dawned that April morning
Blue skies bade us haste away
Where the flower of Scottish football
Meant to show their might that day.
East and West from every quarter
Happy hearts came trooping in.
Till the gates of sunny Ibrox
Close on the great crowd within

Ne'er a thought of pending danger
All are eager for the fray
Quip and jest and friendly jostle
While the waiting time away
Hark! Is that a sound of creaking?
Timid ones grow pale with fear
But the thought is soon forgotten
The contending teams appear.

Free and fast the game is raging
Scotland's sons are pressing sore;
On the tiptoe of excitement
All expect them soon to score
Then is heard a mighty uproar
'God have mercy' someone cried;
Panic-stricken, there's a stampede
Which all human power defies

High above the seething tumult
What an awful sight is seen
Only a great gap remaining
Where the cheerful crowd had been.

Down below are dead and dying,
Mangled forms are all around,
Broken-limbed, and bruised and bleeding;
Like a shambles is the ground.

Willing hands, their hearts nigh failing,
Go to work with tender care,
Till the long, long list of injured
Of their help receive a share.
Brightly dawned that April morning
Blackest night has been the close;
Our sympathy is with the suffering,
Rest the dead in sweet repose.

— RANGERS' TRIPLE CROWNS: 1978 —

For the second time in three years Rangers captured the treble as Jock Wallace wrote himself into the record books as the only Ibrox manager to win two trebles – a feat that only Jock Stein, to this day, has also achieved. Remarkably, this came after a desperately disappointing 1976/77 campaign that drew a total blank.

The introduction of new talent in the summer of 1977 in the shape of Robert Russell from Shettleston Juniors, Gordon Smith from Kilmarnock and Davie Cooper from Clydebank gave the Light Blues an infusion of class that, allied to the skill of Tommy McLean and Derek Johnstone, proved to be much too good for the competition in Scotland.

The championship success was even more extraordinary given that Rangers suffered defeat in their opening two fixtures, 1–3 at Aberdeen and 0–2 at home to Hibernian. However, the season turned around in a remarkable Old Firm encounter at Ibrox on 10th September when the home side overturned a two-goal interval deficit to win 3–2 with two goals from Smith and one from Johnstone. One month later League Cup holders Aberdeen were swept away in the third round of the same competition as Rangers destroyed the Dons 6–1 with Smith notching a hat-trick.

Aberdeen's manager was none other than a certain Billy McNeill, former Celtic legend, who said after the game that Wallace's men had put on the finest display he had ever seen from any Rangers team. Most certainly, the Rangers performance was the finest seen at Ibrox since the days of the early 1960s, of Jim Baxter and Ian McMillan.

Rangers' assault on the League Cup almost ran aground at the semi-final stage when the 'Gers trailed lower division side Forfar Athletic 1–2 at Hampden with just seven minutes remaining, only to be saved from another ignominy of Berwick proportions by a Derek Parlane header. A 5–2 win after extra time saw Rangers qualify for an Old Firm final confrontation, in which the final scoreline of 2–1 to the Light Blues, again after extra time, did not reflect their superiority.

At one time Rangers held a commanding lead in the title race over nearest challengers Aberdeen, but a long unbeaten run from the Pittodrie men saw them reduce the gap at the top to a single point. The Ibrox men steadied just in time, winning their last four games, including a crucial double header against third-placed Dundee United, to clinch their third championship success in four years with a 2–0 home win over Motherwell.

One week later the Ibrox men faced Aberdeen in the Scottish FA Cup Final at Hampden, winning more comfortably than the 2–1 result would suggest through goals from Alex MacDonald and Derek Johnstone.

In the European Cup Winners' Cup, Rangers defeated Young Boys of Berne before being eliminated by Dutch side Twente Enschede, in a tie that came too early in the season for the new Rangers.

While the season was one of great success it was also touched by tragedy with the death of winger Bobby McKean who was found dead in his garage on 15 March 1978 – just three days before the League Cup Final. Rangers did *not* apply for a postponement, and the match went ahead on the scheduled date.

At the end of the season the club was rocked to its foundations with the shock resignation of manager Jock Wallace, to be succeeded by club captain John Greig. In a summer of change in the domestic game Celtic sacked Jock Stein after a disastrous season in which they failed to qualify for Europe. He was followed in the Parkhead hot seat by Aberdeen boss Billy McNeil, who was himself succeeded by Alex Ferguson of St Mirren as a new chapter was about to be written in the annals of Scottish football.

Leading appearance makers: Davie Cooper and Gordon Smith, 52 games
Leading goalscorer: Derek Johnstone, 38 goals

— RANGERS MANAGERS: GRAEME SOUNESS (1986–91) —

The appointment of Graeme Souness as the club's first player-manager in April 1986 revolutionised Scottish football. He turned the club around at a time in the mid-1980s when times were desperate.

Souness's name and reputation helped to attract international stars to Glasgow from England and abroad as transfer records were consistently broken. Four league titles followed in the next five years as did four League Cups. There were outstanding victories over Dynamo Kiev and Górnik Zabrze in the European Cup of 1987/88 but injury problems, a 44-game league campaign and the ineligibility of several key players signed after the European transfer deadline all proved costly in a quarter-final elimination at the hands of Steaua Bucharest. Rangers under Souness were never so close again and the introduction of the UEFA regulations of no more than three non-nationals persuaded the Ibrox manager that he would never achieve the ultimate goal as Rangers boss. He left for Liverpool in April 1991 but failed to replicate his Glasgow success at Anfield, winning just the FA Cup in 1992. In later years he managed Southampton, Blackburn Rovers and Newcastle United in the Premiership as well as Torino and Benfica.

Graeme Souness's honours
League championship: 1986/87, 1988/89, 1989/90, 1990/91
Scottish League Cup: 1986/87, 1987/88, 1988/89, 1990/91

— GREAT EUROPEAN NIGHTS AT IBROX 9 —

Rangers 1   **Ajax 3**
A MacDonald   Rep
                     Cruyff
                     Haan

1972/73 European Super Cup, first leg
16th January 1973
Attendance: 60,000

It all started with an invitation to Amsterdam giants Ajax (European Cup holders for the two previous seasons) to visit Ibrox in January 1973 as part of Rangers' centenary celebrations (albeit they were being marked one year late). The Dutch club were only too willing to accept, and proposed a return match in Amsterdam. Thus the European Super Cup was born with UEFA readily adopting the idea, and the Rangers-Ajax meeting of 1972–73 is now accepted as the inaugural fixture in the series.

Ibrox Stadium was awash with nostalgia on the evening of the home leg, with the colours of every club Rangers had faced in European competition displayed by pupils from local schools Bellahouston Academy and Govan High School. At the interval, both of Europe's two premier trophies were paraded before the 60,000 spectators by pupils from Hyndland Secondary School – one wonders when the European Cup will make a reappearance in Govan?

Glasgow's Lord Provost William Gray was introduced to both teams prior to kick-off – hard as it is to believe nowadays, Glasgow's leading citizen in 1973 had Light Blue leanings! Legendary former player Andy Cunningham ceremoniously kicked off, and the home side could have done with the presence of some of the greats who had graced the Ibrox turf over the years, for Ajax were without question the finest club side in the world – Johan Cruyff, Johan Neeskens, Ruud Krol, Johnny Rep, Arie Haan, Arnold and Gerry Muhren were all players of the highest class.

The Dutch masters produced an astonishing opening half

hour, displaying superb football at breathtaking speed, with the magnificent Cruyff at the epicentre. Rangers were not dishonoured however, somehow surviving that spell before succumbing on 35 minutes when Cruyff created the opening goal with a perfectly weighted pass to Rep who drew Peter McCloy off his line before stroking the ball home.

Rangers' response befitted the occasion. Just seven minutes later they scored an equaliser when a long pass from John Greig found Alfie Conn, who in turn released Alex MacDonald to shoot home on the turn from a tight angle off Heinz Stuy's left-hand post from the edge of the area.

The game turned on the stroke of half-time, however, with a superlative goal scored by the majestic Cruyff. It was one of the finest ever seen at the old stadium, as the Ajax number 14 sped towards the home goal pursued by Derek Johnstone. DJ seemed to have closed his opponent down, blocking his road to goal, only to fall victim to the classic Cruyff double-shuffle – a sudden drop in pace with the ball still under absolute control whilst the Ranger slithered helplessly past him. The Dutch maestro doubled back, swivelled, and as Tom Forsyth raced in to help, struck a vicious left-foot shot into the net.

Ibrox rose to acclaim a genius.

Ajax were in command, although Rangers pressed hard after the interval with Derek Parlane, John Greig and Tommy McLean all coming close while one superb Johnstone run deserved better than to end with a shot inches wide. The classic sucker punch was struck at 76 minutes when that man Cruyff found Barry Hulshoff. He touched on to Haan who evaded Johnstone to crash home a great shot.

In truth Ajax had been a class apart, and in a classic encounter the home side won the return in Amsterdam 3–2.

Rangers team: McCloy; Jardine, Mathieson; Greig, Johnstone, Smith; Conn (McLean), Forsyth, Parlane, A MacDonald, Young

— RANGERS LEGENDS: RICHARD GOUGH (1987–98) —

Richard Gough: led by example

Rangers' first £1 million signing, Richard Gough was club captain during seven of the 'Nine-In-a-Row' seasons, and for that reason alone he deserves his place amongst the all-time Rangers Greats.

He arrived at Ibrox via a circuitous route in October 1987. Stockholm-born to a Swedish mother and Scottish father, Gough spent his formative years in South Africa. At the age of 18 he played a trial match for Rangers but failed to impress. He fared better at Dundee United under manager Jim McLean, and in six years at Tannadice won international recognition as well as, remarkably, a league championship winners' medal in 1982/83. He might have been one of Graeme Souness's first signings early in 1986 but McLean refused to countenance the transfer, and Gough signed for Tottenham Hotspur instead. At White Hart Lane he captained Spurs at the 1987 FA Cup Final against Coventry City.

One year on from their initial approach Rangers finally got their man when Spurs accepted a £1.1 million transfer fee. He made an immediate impact with the Light Blue legions when, in his home debut against Celtic on 17th October 1987, he scored a last-minute equaliser as nine-man Rangers fought back from a two-goal deficit to draw 2–2. Another crucial goal in an Old Firm encounter was the extra-time winner that ensured a 2–1 triumph in the 1990/91 League Cup Final.

A dedicated and disciplined professional, Gough would prove to be sound value for money over the next decade. He succeeded Terry Butcher as captain, and led the club to outstanding success throughout the 1990s. The only player to win all nine league championship winners' medals during the historic Nine-in-a-Row, he added six League Cup and three Scottish Cup winners' medals for good measure.

In his younger days Gough was a versatile defender, able to play at full back or in the central defensive position that eventually became his rightful place at the heart of Walter Smith's all-conquering team of the 1990s. Fit and athletic, he was strong in the air and secure on the ground, his timing and distribution out of the danger area first class. He was an intelligent, thoughtful, courageous and consistent player and a first-class representative for the club. On and off the park he led by example in a decade of outstanding success for the club, the camaraderie and team spirit of that Rangers squad being testament to his leadership qualities.

Qualified to play for both Sweden and South Africa, Gough chose instead the country of his father Charles, who had played for Charlton Athletic in the 1960s. He played 61 times for Scotland, a total that would have surely been much greater but for a fall-out with successive international managers Andy Roxburgh and Craig Brown.

After his Ibrox days were over, he played in the USA for Kansas City Wiz and San Jose Earthquake before returning to the UK, to play for both Nottingham Forest and Everton (under Walter Smith) in the Premiership leading many Rangers fans to ponder whether he had left Govan prematurely.

A brief spell in management with Livingston saw him successfully retain the Almondvale club's Scottish Premier League status – no mean feat in the light of subsequent events – before he returned to the United States for family reasons.

Richard Gough factfile
Born Stockholm, Sweden, 5th April 1962
Appearances: 397
Goals: 32
Full international appearances while at Rangers: 28 caps for Scotland
Honours:
League championship: 1982/83 (Dundee United), 1988/89, 1989/90, 1990/91, 1991/92, 1992/93, 1993/94, 1994/95, 1995/96, 1996/97
Scottish FA Cup: 1992, 1993, 1996
Scottish League Cup: 1987/88, 1988/89, 1990/91, 1992/93, 1993/94, 1996/97
Player of the Year: 1989

— RANGERS MANAGERS: WALTER SMITH (1991–98; 2006–PRESENT) —

Walter Smith was assistant manager to Graeme Souness for five years before succeeding him in April 1991, having previously served in a similar capacity under Jim McLean at Dundee United where he played a key role in that club's astonishing league championship success in 1982/83.

Of all Rangers' managers only William Wilton and Bill Struth have won more titles than 'Wattie'. He led the club to 'Nine-In-A-Row', achieving six of the nine. Smith left Rangers in 1998 after just missing out on a tenth consecutive championship, going on to manage Everton and the Scottish national side before returning to Ibrox in January 2007. The following season was a truly remarkable one as Rangers were robbed of the league championship through a combination of fixture manipulation and key refereeing decisions. That wrong was righted in 2008/09.

During Smith's two periods in office there were two outstanding European campaigns. In the inaugural Champions League of 1992/93 an unbeaten run of ten games saw the Light Blues come agonisingly close to a European Cup Final, being denied only by an Olympique Marseille side that was later convicted in the French courts of corruption. One of the games

Walter Smith: trophy collector

cited as evidence against the French club was a 1–0 victory over Club Brugge that was crucial to denying Rangers a place in the Munich Final. In 2007/08, after his return to Ibrox, Smith remarkably led the club to a fourth European final before losing to a superb Zenit Saint Petersburg in Manchester.

Walter Smith's honours
League championship: 1991/92, 1992/93, 1993/94, 1994/95, 1995/96, 1996/97, 2008/09
Scottish Cup: 1992, 1993, 1996, 2008, 2009
Scottish League Cup: 1992/93, 1993/94, 1996/97, 2007/08

— RECORD ATTENDANCE —

On 2nd January 1939 a record attendance at Ibrox of 118,730 saw Rangers defeat Celtic 2–1. The crowd figure is also a British record for a league game that stands to this day and will surely never be bettered. Incredibly an additional estimated 30,000 spectators were locked out.

— CLUB SONGS —

As with most clubs today, the fans who pack Ibrox to capacity at almost every game have a varied selection of popular songs in their repertoire. The most well-known would of course be *Follow Follow*, but that was not always the case. Before the outbreak of war in 1939 the best-loved song amongst Rangers fans was *The Bonnie Wells O'Wearie*. Amongst many older 'Gers fans who were present at the historic 1928 Scottish Cup Final one of the fondest memories (apart of course from the result – a 4–0 thrashing of Celtic) was of *The Bonnie Wells O' Wearie* ringing around Hampden during the dying minutes of the game. Regular singing at matches, though, is a relatively modern phenomenon – dating from the late 1960s onwards.

Today of course a wide range of chants and songs fill the air at almost every football match, some more savoury than others. Amongst Rangers supporters other popular ditties include *Every Other Saturday*, *Who's That Team They Call The Rangers?*, *The Famous Glasgow Rangers*, *The Blue Sea of Ibrox*, *The Bouncy* and other traditional folk songs.

— GREAT EUROPEAN NIGHTS AT IBROX 10 —

Rangers 2   **Juventus 0**
A MacDonald
Smith

1978/79 European Cup, first round, second leg
29th September 1978
Attendance: 44,000

When John Greig succeeded Jock Wallace in the Ibrox hot seat he inherited a team that had just won the treble but had failed to make an impact in Europe. Prospects of a prolonged European run appeared grim when the Scottish champions were paired with Italian giants Juventus in the opening round of the 1978/79 European Cup. The Italian champions are always a difficult prospect at any time, but this Juventus team was regarded as the cream of Europe, containing as it did no fewer than nine players in the Italian side that had reached the World Cup semi-finals in Argentina that very summer. Indeed, it had been a tournament the 'Azzurri' might well have won, given that they defeated the hosts and eventual winners in the group stages.

In the first leg, played in Turin, Juve won 1–0, leaving the tie in the balance for the Ibrox return. The Italian champions arrived in Glasgow exuding confidence despite their narrow lead, and there were many Light Blue followers who doubted their team's ability to overhaul the one-goal deficit, given that no Ibrox side had ever overturned a first-leg loss in Europe. It was surely inconceivable that they could do so against the best that Serie A could offer. Yet the young Rangers manager would outwit Juventus coach Giovanni Trappatoni, shrewdly altering his formation by switching Tommy McLean from right wing to left.

A crowd of 44,000 packed a stadium under reconstruction, with the Copland Road end a building site. The night would go down in Ibrox folklore as Rangers produced one of the finest performances of any Scottish club in Europe. A cleverly worked free kick unlocked the 'catenaccio' defence in 17 minutes – Gordon Smith's shot being punched out by goalkeeper Dino Zoff (Italy's 1982 World Cup-winning captain) only for Alex McDonald to head home from close range. The home side were now dictating the tactical direction of the play, and added a second on 68 minutes when a Robert Russell free kick was met by Smith – his header soaring beyond the outstretched Zoff into the far corner of the net.

Juve were stunned – but fought to the end. Rangers, however, held on for a memorable triumph that restored the club's good name throughout Europe. Another stunning win over PSV Eindhoven followed in the next round, but just when it appeared that the European Cup might be Ibrox-bound, a severe winter led to fixture congestion and that, combined with an injury crisis, cost the Ibrox men dear, being eliminated by Köln in the last eight.

Rangers team: McCloy; Jardine, A Forsyth; T Forsyth, Jackson, A MacDonald; McLean, Russell, Parlane, Johnstone, Smith

— RANGERS' TRIPLE CROWNS: 1993 —

Of all the Nine-in-a-Row campaigns, perhaps the one most fondly recalled is that of season 1992/93 when Rangers not only won the treble for a fifth time, but also came within one game of reaching the UEFA Champions League Final.

Five in a row was the main aim for all with Light Blue leanings as the season unfolded – a feat the Ibrox men had not achieved, excluding the war years, for more than six decades.

1992/93 would go into the history books as arguably the finest in the club's history. At its heart was an unprecedented 44-game unbeaten run in all competitions that ran from 15th August to 20th March. The main challenge to Light Blue domination throughout came from Aberdeen – the Dons finished second in the league, nine points adrift, and would reach both domestic cup finals. The League Cup Final was won 2–1 deep into extra time courtesy of a Gary Smith own goal, whilst the Scottish FA Cup Final, played at Celtic Park due to reconstruction work at Hampden, also ended 2–1 to the Ibrox men with strikes from Neil Murray and Mark Hateley.

The key to the title success was a run of 11 consecutive wins early on and key wins over Aberdeen and Celtic that effectively nullified the main opposition. Single goal wins at Parkhead and Pittodrie, in November and February respectively, courtesy of goals from Ian Durrant and a trademark Mark Hateley header underlined the resilience and character of a squad that brimmed with talent. The championship was clinched four games from home at Broomfield Park, Airdrie with Gary McSwegan notching the only goal of the game.

In Europe, Rangers came agonisingly closing to making it four trophies for the season. Despite the imposition of the maximum three non-national ruling by UEFA (a regulation that penalised Rangers almost more than any other club) the defeat of Danish champions Lyngby and English champions Leeds United ensured qualification for the inaugural UEFA Champions League where Rangers remained unbeaten in a group comprising Olympique Marseille, Brugge, and CSKA Moscow. Two titanic struggles with the French champions ended all square – only for

Marseille to progress to the Munich final following a 1–0 in Belgium in their final group fixture. They went on to secure the Champions Cup with a 1–0 win over AC Milan, the goalscorer a certain Basile Boli who would join Rangers one year later.

That summer, investigations began into Olympique Marseille and their president Bernard Tapie following accusations from French club Valenciennes that they had been bribed to lose a crucial league fixture. The case went to the French courts where Marseille and Tapie were found guilty of bribery and corruption, the club relegated and their president imprisoned for five years. Amongst the fixtures cited in the courts was the win at Brugge that denied Rangers. Justice had been seen to be done in the French courts – but had been denied to Rangers.

A 64-game season that incorporated a ridiculous and crippling 44-game league campaign, ten European Cup and five apiece in League and Scottish Cups was a record number of games played by the club, surpassed only by the total in 2007/08.

Leading appearance maker: David Robertson, 58 games
Leading goalscorer: Ally McCoist, 49 goals

— A CHEQUE WILL DO NICELY, THANKS —

When Alan Hutton moved to Tottenham from Rangers early in 2008 he did so for a club record £9 million. Including Hutton, the departing players to most benefit the Ibrox coffers are:

Fee	Year	Player	Club
£9m	2008	Alan Hutton	Tottenham
£8.5m	2001	Giovanni van Bronckhurst	Arsenal
£8m	2005	Jean-Alain Boumsong	Newcastle
£7.5m	2003	Barry Ferguson	Blackburn
£6.75m	2002	Tore André Flo	Sunderland

— HISTORY OF THE GROUNDS: IBROX STADIUM —

By the late 1890s Rangers had outgrown First Ibrox and required a bigger, grander stage in which to perform in front of their legion of fans. The solution the club hit upon was simply to build a new stadium alongside the existing one.

Ibrox mark II was an entirely new concept in football stadia designed by architect Archibald Leitch. Covering 14.5 acres, an ornate three-storey pavilion that could accommodate 1,000 spectators in the south-east corner of the ground, a grandstand seating 4,500 spectators (with a roof transported from First Ibrox) and an enclosure in front that could house an additional 10,000, the stadium was a vast improvement on its neighbour. Opposite the grandstand stood the Bovril Stand, a covered enclosure that ran the full length of the pitch. The new ground was opened on 30th December 1899 with a 3-1 Inter-City League win over Hearts with a Wilkie hat-trick in front of a 12,000 audience.

The sporting press acclaimed the new ground – "a Colosseum of football" and "the finest football ground in the world" were just two of the descriptions of the first football ground to be built on the amphitheatre principle. Within two years the capacity had risen to 75,000 – but the Ibrox Disaster of 1902 (see page 15) necessitated a rethink and the need to rebuild on safer lines. The original structure had provided for wooden tiers on scaffolding and an iron framework at either end, but following 1902 the design incorporated solid earth embankments on the terraces, to be replaced much later by concrete. In 1904 Rangers purchased the ground from the Hinshelwood Trust for the princely sum of £15,000, thus owning their home for the first time. By 1905 Ibrox had been rebuilt to accommodate 25,000, then by 1910 63,000, taking on the vast oval shape that would endure until 1978.

The club's ambitions knew no limits in the following years – at the end of the First World War the capacity had increased to 80,000 and during the 1920s as the club regained the dominant position in Scottish football it had enjoyed at the turn of the century they set about building the finest grandstand in all of Britain.

Designed once again by Archibald Leitch, this would prove to be his finest creation, seating 10,500 spectators. It featured an imposing red-brick facade in mock neoclassical style with arched windows on its upper floors and at each end the club crest with its lion rampant shield and *Aye Ready* motto emblazoned in blue and gold mosaic. The entrance hall and main staircase were in marble, while the corridors and boardroom were panelled in the finest wood. A magnificently crenellated press box (sadly long gone) was positioned on the roof of the grandstand and massive blue wrought-iron gates stood at either end of the stand. As a final touch the distinctive Leitch criss-cross balcony wall was added at the front of the new stand. It survives to this day, as it does at Everton's Goodison Park and Portsmouth's Fratton Park.

The structure was a clear statement of superiority and supremacy over all other competitors. It was opened on 1st January 1929 with an emphatic 3-0 win over Celtic. In the years that followed art deco lamps, the trophy room and the Alan Morton portrait were all added to Scotland's finest stadium. In 1980 the final accolade was bestowed on Archibald Leitch's work when his grandstand became a listed building.

The 1971 disaster (see page 81) led to a major rethink on safety and comfort. Seven years later redevelopment work changed the shape of the ground from oval to rectangular as the vast terraces were swept away and in their place three modern stands were built on the 'goalpost' design at a cost of £10 million. In later years the ground became all-seated, a third tier was added to Leitch's Main Stand and the corners were filled in, linking up the Copland Road, Govan and Broomloan Road Stands.

Today Ibrox Stadium is a 51,000-capacity arena that is without question the finest in Scotland and one of Europe's best.

— GREAT EUROPEAN NIGHTS AT IBROX 11 —

Rangers 2   Dynamo Kiev 0
Falco
McCoist

1987/88 European Cup, first round, second leg
30th September 1987
Attendance: 44,500

With the championship secured in Graeme Souness's first season as player-manager, Rangers entered the European Cup for the first time in nine years. The first round draw could not have been any tougher – Dynamo Kiev, champions of the USSR. It would be the club's first visit to the Soviet Union in competitive European football, although they had undertaken a memorable, unbeaten tour in 1962.

Kiev were a side of the highest quality, the vast majority of their squad forming the national side of the USSR that would go on to win Olympic Gold in Seoul the following year, as well as being runners-up in the 1988 European Championships. Two of their stars, Oleg Kuznetsov and Alexei Mikhailichenko, would in later years join Rangers.

A 1–0 defeat in Kiev, with only a handful of 'Gers fans present, left all to play for at Ibrox. Controversy swirled around the Rangers stadium two weeks later when, with the Soviet champions having trained the previous evening (as per UEFA regulations) on the normal–sized Ibrox pitch, the touchlines were brought in on both wings in a bid to negate the pace of Kiev wingers Vasily Rats and Oleg Blokhin.

No matter the ethics of such a tactic, and it was certainly within the laws of the game as Kiev found out when they checked it out post-match, Rangers could never within their wildest dreams have imagined that they would receive the gift that the visitors presented to them after 24 minutes. An attack had broken down with the ball safely in the hands of goalkeeper Victor Chanov. His clearance from hand produced an error of schoolboy proportions – striking Sergei Baltacha on the backside, it fell perfectly for Ally McCoist who slipped the ball into the path of Mark Falco who coolly stroked the ball into the net.

The aggregate scores were now level, and as Rangers controlled the game the capacity crowd began to dream of an outstanding European scalp. The second goal arrived five minutes into the second half when a Trevor Francis cross was headed on by Falco to McCoist who guided his header into the corner of the net.

Teams of the quality of Dynamo Kiev are not prone to accepting defeat readily – and this night was no different as the Ukrainians piled on the pressure in the closing stages, using their pace to maximum effect in an effort to turn the home defence. The closing quarter appeared to last forever for the Light Blue legions, but a solid Rangers defence held out on one of the great Ibrox nights.

Rangers' fans hopes of claiming the ultimate prize, though, were dashed by Steaua Bucharest at the quarter-final stage, in part due to some managerial idiosyncrasies on the transfer front.

Rangers team: C Woods; Nicholl, Phillips; McGregor, Souness, Butcher; Francis (Fleck), Falco, McCoist, Durrant, Cohen (Kirkwood)

— ALL ROADS LEAD TO IBROX —

When in 1887 Rangers, removing from Kinning Park, announced their intention to move to a new ground at Ibrox there was considerable debate in the sporting press of the day. Were the 'Light Blues' making a mistake in moving "out of the city into the country"? The district of Ibrox was at the time on the outskirts of the city, but the club rightly anticipated the spread westward of the city's growing population and the extension of Glasgow's transport system.

Transport officials were amongst the official guests at the opening of First Ibrox, and it was soon clear that the new ground would be well served in terms of links to the city centre. The Joint Line Railway Company ran trains from St Enoch Station to Ibrox Station for just one and a half-pennies whilst the Vale of Clyde Tramway Company laid on new tramcars to run from Paisley Road Toll to Copland Road with a branch line running on match-days to the gates of the park for one penny or all the way by horse-drawn brake from Queen Street in the city centre for twopence.

The proximity of the River Clyde might have proved a barrier to attracting spectators, but the existence of ferries and the river steamers which the Clutha Company proposed to run for the convenience of Rangers' home games soon overcame that potential problem

In 1896 the Glasgow District Underground was opened with a station at Copland Road (subsequently renamed Ibrox in the late 1970s), thus making the Rangers ground by far the most accessible of the city's football stadia. Ibrox Railway Station, on the line from Glasgow St Enoch to Paisley Canal Street was located at the junction of Paisley Road West and Broomloan Road (the site today of a petrol station). In later years a 'platform halt' (for use on matchdays) was added on Edmiston Drive, almost directly opposite the present location of the Rangers Supporters' Association Social Club. The railway line actually ran behind the North Terracing (site today of the Govan Stand) and in the 1930s plans were drawn up to extend the ground to a capacity of some 200,000 with the proposals including the construction of a double-decker grandstand above the North Terrace with a new 'platform halt' built to allow direct access to the stand. The plan was not implemented, though.

The Glasgow tramway system survived until 1962 when its removal was just one of a series of disastrous planning decisions that blighted the city at that time. The railway line was closed by the Beeching cuts of the 1960s. Today, of course, the trams may have gone, as has the railway line, but the subway survives.

— SCOTTISH FA CUP TRIUMPHS —

Rangers have won the Scottish FA Cup on 32 occasions as follows:

Year	Opponents	Venue	Attendance	Result
1894	Celtic	2nd Hampden	17,000	3–1
1897	Dumbarton	2nd Hampden	15,000	5–1
1898	Kilmarnock	2nd Hampden	14,000	2–0
1903	Hearts	Celtic Park	30,000	1–1
	Hearts (r)	Celtic Park	35,000	0–0
	Hearts (r)	Celtic Park	35,000	2–0
1928	Celtic	Hampden Park	118,115	4–0
1930	Partick Thistle	Hampden Park	107,457	0–0
	Partick Thistle (r)	Hampden Park	103,688	2–1
1932	Kilmarnock	Hampden Park	111,982	1–1
	Kilmarnock (r)	Hampden Park	105,695	3–0
1934	St Mirren	Hampden Park	113,403	5–0
1935	Hamilton Academical	Hampden Park	87,740	2–1
1936	Third Lanark	Hampden Park	88,859	1–0
1948	Morton	Hampden Park	131,975	1–1
	Morton (r)	Hampden Park	133,750	1–0
1949	Clyde	Hampden Park	120,162	4–1
1950	East Fife	Hampden Park	120,015	3–0
1953	Aberdeen	Hampden Park	129,762	1–1
	Aberdeen (r)	Hampden Park	113,700	1–0
1960	Kilmarnock	Hampden Park	108,017	2–0
1962	St Mirren	Hampden Park	127,940	2–0
1963	Celtic	Hampden Park	129,643	1–1
	Celtic (r)	Hampden Park	120,273	3–0
1964	Dundee	Hampden Park	120,982	3–1
1966	Celtic	Hampden Park	126,599	0–0
	Celtic (r)	Hampden Park	98,202	1–0
1973	Celtic	Hampden Park	122,714	3–2
1976	Hearts	Hampden Park	85,354	3–1
1978	Aberdeen	Hampden Park	61,563	2–1
1979	Hibernian	Hampden Park	50,610	0–0
	Hibernian (r)	Hampden Park	33,504	0–0
	Hibernian (r)	Hampden Park	30,602	3–2

1981	Dundee United	Hampden Park	53,346	0–0
	Dundee United (r)	Hampden Park	43,099	4–1
1992	Airdrieonians	Hampden Park	44,045	2–1
1993	Aberdeen	Celtic Park	50,715	2–1
1996	Hearts	Hampden Park	37,730	5–1
1999	Celtic	Hampden Park	51,746	1–0
2000	Aberdeen	Hampden Park	50,865	4–0
2002	Celtic	Hampden Park	51,138	3–2
2003	Dundee	Hampden Park	47,136	1–0
2008	Queen of the South	Hampden Park	48,821	3–2
2009	Falkirk	Hampden Park	50,956	1–0

— GREAT EUROPEAN NIGHTS AT IBROX 12 —

Rangers 2 **Leeds United 1**
McCoist McAllister
Lukic og

1992/93 European Cup, second round, first leg
21st October 1992
Attendance: 44,000

Having eliminated Danish champions Lyngby in the opening round, when Rangers were paired with English champions Leeds United the stakes could scarcely have been any higher, with entry to the inaugural UEFA Champions League at stake. The Yorkshire club were more than fortunate to still be in the tournament – defeated on away goals by VfB Stuttgart (0–3, 4–1) they suddenly found themselves reinstated by UEFA when it became apparent that the Germans had breached the regulation that decreed that clubs were barred from using more than three non-nationals in any one game. The result of the second leg was amended to one of 3–0, necessitating a one-off third match in Barcelona which Leeds won 2–1.

Controversy raged when both clubs refused to countenance the allocation of tickets for away supporters – a ban that the two sets of fans got around by supplying briefs to each other.

Leeds were formidable opponents – included in their squad was old friend Gordon Strachan (formerly of Aberdeen and Manchester United), the mercurial Eric Cantona, Scottish international midfielder Gary McAllister and future Ranger Rod Wallace.

The tie was inevitably dubbed 'The Battle of Britain' by the media – and within 60 seconds of the start Ibrox was silenced by a quite stunning 18-yard strike from McAllister after a Strachan corner had been partially cleared.

For 20 minutes Leeds dominated play, but Rangers however had perceived a weakness in visiting goalkeeper John Lukic, in that he was susceptible to the cross ball. A succession of corners finally paid dividend when he fisted Durrant's inswinger into his own net on 21 minutes. Before the interval the Light Blues had the lead when another Durrant corner saw Lukic parry McPherson's effort only for McCoist, ever the predator, to convert the rebound.

The noise and tension was unbearable, with the atmosphere on one of the great European nights electric. The second half produced no more goals, and Rangers had a narrow 2–1 lead to take to Elland Road where, on a memorable night in Yorkshire, Rangers repeated their 2–1 win, opening the door to a never-to-be-forgotten Champions League campaign.

Rangers team: Goram; McCall, D Robertson; Gough, McPherson, Brown; Steven (Huistra), I Ferguson, McCoist, Hateley, Durrant

— PAYING THE ULTIMATE PRICE —

Five Rangers players were killed during the Great War:

- David Murray, a private in the Seaforth Highlanders, was killed in action on 6th October 1915, and is buried at Lapugnoy Military Cemetery, France.
- James Speirs, a second lieutenant in the Cameron Highlanders, was killed in action in Belgium on 20th August 1917 and is buried at Dochy Farm New British Cemetery, Zonnebeke (7km north/east of Ypres), Belgium.
- John Fleming, a corporal in the Cameron Highlanders died, aged 26, in Richmond Camp, Yorkshire on 21st March 1916. He is buried at Inveresk Parish Church, Midlothian.
- Alex Barrie, a corporal in the Highland Light Infantry, was killed in action on 1st October 1918 and is buried at Flesquieres Hill British Cemetery North, France.
- Walter Tull, who was not only the first black player to sign for Rangers, but also the first black commissioned officer in the British Army, was killed at the Second Battle of the Somme. Like many others who were killed in action during the First World War there is no grave for the Ranger. However, his name is inscribed on the War Memorial of the Faubourg-Amiens War Cemetery and Memorial at Arras, France, and in the Commonwealth War Graves Commission Roll of Honour for the City of Glasgow Memorial. His name also appears on the Roll of Honour at Claremont Street Methodist Church, where he was a member.

The loss of life of those with Ibrox links extended beyond the playing staff, for the sons of directors William Craig and William R Danskin were also killed in action, and the son of director Walter Crichton was wounded.

In addition, Rangers players John Clarke, Tommy Muirhead, Finlay Speedie, Jimmy Low, John Bovill, Willie Kivlichan, James Paterson, John McCulloch and James Galt were wounded in action. Jack Bovill suffered from the effects of a gas shell explosion that killed a comrade standing just beside him.

— SNEAKING BEHIND THE IRON CURTAIN —

Mainly because of the expense involved, very few Rangers fans followed the club away in the early days of European competition. Two exceptions were Ross Bowie and Joe Welsh, a pair of supporters who were frequently paying guests on the club's official flights.

In 1959 Rangers were drawn in the European Cup against Red Star Bratislava of Czechoslovakia, then a Soviet satellite with strict visa requirements for visitors from the West. Rangers duly applied to the Czechoslovakian Embassy in London for visas for their official party but when the documentation was returned to manager Scot Symon he quickly realised that Bowie and Welsh had not been issued with the necessary papers.

No reason was given for the exclusion, or indeed whether it was a simple oversight or otherwise, but there was little that could be done about it – or so it seemed.

However, at the last minute and very much on a whim, Bowie and Welsh (both sadly no longer with us) decided to fly to Vienna, just 25 miles from Bratislava. Hiring a car in the Austrian capital, they drove to the Czechoslovakian border on the day before the game in an attempt to somehow be granted permission to enter Czechoslovakia. Armed guards and blank stares greeted the two Scots who vainly tried to explain that "football" and "Glasgow Rangers" was the purpose of their visit, the universal passport that should open all doors. Sadly, however, the only answer forthcoming was a request for "papers" which effectively meant visa as well as passport.

Undaunted, the intrepid duo turned back to Vienna only to return the next day, the day of the game, when crucially a new set of border guards were on duty, including most importantly at least one who was himself a football fan. There remained a language barrier, but gifts of a Rangers pennant and lapel badge together with a bottle of Scotch whisky somehow persuaded a sympathetic guard to allow them to cross the border without visas with the stipulation, by way of sign language, that they return by 6pm.

The pair drove straight to the stadium in Bratislava, where a new problem presented itself – a lack of match tickets with kick-off rapidly approaching. This was a problem soon overcome by boldly walking straight up to the main entrance where, by dint of their Rangers' blazers and ties, they were assumed to be club officials and waved straight through to trackside where an incredulous Scot Symon greeted them.

The pair watched the game (a 1–1 draw which gave Rangers a 5–4 aggregate victory) from the trainer's bench, before setting off back to the border at the final whistle. They made good time and, passing through a small village not far from the border, it was decided that a quick beer was the order of the day.

Who should our two friends find in the tavern but the selfsame border guard who had permitted them passage – and a convivial evening was spent toasting Rangers, Red Star, Robert Burns, and so on. It was well past midnight before Bowie and Welsh were spirited back out of Czechoslovakia to the West – and a day to remember was at an end.

— GREAT EUROPEAN NIGHTS AT IBROX 13 —

Rangers 2   Parma 0
Vidmar
Reyna

1999/2000 Champions League, third qualifying round, first leg
11th August 1999
Attendance: 49,263

Having regained the league title in Dick Advocaat's first season as Rangers manager, the Ibrox men eliminated FC Haka of Finland in the second qualifying round of the Champions League, only to find themselves obliged to face Parma of Italy for the second time in eight months. The prospect was an intimidating one as Parma had eliminated the Scots from the previous season's UEFA Cup, and retained a star-studded cast of the calibre of Gianluigi Buffon, Dino Baggio, Herman Crespo, Juan Sebastián

Verón, Fabio Cannavaro and Lilian Thuram. This time, though, it was to prove different and become perhaps Dick Advocaat's finest hour.

To general astonishment Rangers defeated the Italians 2–0 at Ibrox with goals from Tony Vidmar and Claudio Reyna. Indeed, Giovanni van Bronckhorst had an outstanding chance late in the game to make the first game lead ever more formidable, but blazed his shot over the bar, deep into the Copland Road Stand. Parma had been certainly handicapped by being reduced to ten men in the first half when two yellow cards saw Cannavaro taking the walk of shame. In the second leg Rangers limited the Italians to a 1–0 win, and thus qualified for the Champions League.

Rangers team: Klos; Porrini, Vidmar (Albertz); Amoruso, Moore, B Ferguson; Reyna, Wallace, Mols, Van Bronckhorst, McCann

— GIANT-KILLED! —

Like all big clubs, Rangers have suffered their fair share of cup shocks over the years. Here are ten of the most embarrassing upsets:

Date	Competition	Result
15th Nov 1884	Scottish Cup 4th rd	Arbroath 4 Rangers 3
7th April 1920	Scottish Cup s/f	Albion 2 Rangers 0
15th April 1922	Scottish Cup final	Morton 1 Rangers 0
17th Sept 1949	League Cup q/f	Rangers 2 Cowdenbeath 3
8th Oct 1949	League Cup s/f	East Fife 2 Rangers 1
13th Aug 1958	League Cup group	Raith Rovers 3 Rangers 1
28th Jan 1967	Scottish Cup 1st rd	Berwick 1 Rangers 0
4th Oct 1972	League Cup 2nd rd	Rangers 1 Stenhousemuir 2
31st Jan 1987	Scottish Cup 3rd rd	Rangers 0 Hamilton 1
8th Nov 2006	League Cup q/f	Rangers 0 St Johnstone 2

— GREAT EUROPEAN NIGHTS AT IBROX 14 —

Rangers 5   Sturm Graz 0
Mols
De Boer
Albertz
Van Bronckhurst
Dodds

2000/01 UEFA Champions League Group D
12th September 2000
Attendance: 49,317

The opening match of Champions League Group D in season 2000/01 saw Rangers entertain the Austrians and a 5–0 win was the resounding result. It was one of Rangers' most impressive Champions League performances, distinguished by the superb play of Ronald de Boer, a player of the highest quality who had already sampled Champions League success with Ajax and who joined Rangers from Barcelona. His twin brother, Frank, was also to join the club, four years on. De Boer was one of three big-money signings from the Netherlands secured by Dick Advocaat that season – Fernando Ricksen from AZ Alkmaar and Bert Konterman from Feyenoord were the others, neither of whom, it is fair to say, had the pedigree of de Boer.

The 5–0 win over Sturm Graz was one of the great European nights at Ibrox. Rangers missed a penalty, struck the Graz woodwork twice but it mattered little as goals from Michael Mols, Ronald de Boer (his first for the club), Jörg Albertz, Giovanni van Bronckhorst and Billy Dodds destroyed the visitors. It was the first time that Rangers had won their opening match in a Champions League group.

Sadly, despite following up that victory with an outstanding result in Monaco, Rangers could only finish in third place in the group, continuing their European campaign in the UEFA Cup where they were eliminated by Germany's Kaiserslautern.

Rangers team: Klos; Ricksen, Numan; Amoruso, Konterman, B

Ferguson; Johnston (Kanchelskis), de Boer (McCann), Mols (Dodds), Albertz, van Bronckhorst

— ER, THANK YOUSE BELGIUMS! —

In the early years of European football it was the custom for both teams and officials to attend a post-match banquet, and at the function in Brussels in 1959, held in the Atomium that overlooks the Stade du Heysel, the venue for the infamous 1985 disaster, the Anderlecht president was fulsome in his apologies for the conduct of his players during the tie.

His address was given in three languages (Flemish, French and English) and after his polished performance the Rangers' party had something of a problem – who should reply on behalf of the club? Manager Scot Symon was by nature a shy and reserved character, and was reluctant to take the stand. Future Scotland manager Craig Brown was a young reserve at the time, and it was suggested that as a university student he might say a few words. Eventually, however, it was agreed that Bobby Shearer, as club captain, should speak. His words were thankfully brief and to the point:

I'd like to thank youse Belgiums for all the grub and bevvy. Cheers!

His few words presumably left the hosts to rethink their understanding of the English language.

— NOT QUITE FINISHED —

In a European Cup tie between Rangers and Nice in 1956 English referee Arthur Ellis mistakenly blew for full-time after just 85 minutes. Realising his error, he recalled the players to complete the game. Rangers player Eric Caldow was already in the dressing room and later recalled: "I had my boots off at the time. That was the day of my brother's wedding, and I was best man. I had to rush off back to the reception, but George Young came in and told me to get back on the park – the game hadn't finished."

— RANGERS' TRIPLE CROWNS: 1999 —

Dick Advocaat became the first manager in Scottish football history to win a treble in his first season as manager. He arrived at Ibrox in the summer of 1998 and introduced a 'Dutch Revolution' to the club, introducing players of true international class like Stefan Klos, Arthur Numan and Giovanni van Bronckhorst as all previous transfer records were smashed.

Despite suffering defeat in his opening league fixture at Tynecastle, Advocaat soon had Rangers back in their rightful place as league leaders. Even a heavy 1–5 defeat at Celtic Park in November (Rangers played more than half the game with ten men) whilst unacceptable was no more than a hiccup, as the class and consistency of the Ibrox men shone through.

The League Cup was claimed in November with a 2–1 win over St Johnstone at Celtic Park, and even if the final was less than memorable it was certainly notable as the first trophy won by the Little General. Stéphane Guivarc'h, a World Cup winner with France that summer, had opened the scoring in the final but would not last the season in Govan. Jörg Albertz netted the other.

Rangers had failed to defeat Celtic in the first three Old Firm meetings of the Advocaat era – but the Dutch manager would soon make up for lost time by the season's close. The league championship was regained in the most dramatic of fashions on 2nd May with a stunning 3–0 win at Parkhead, two goals from Neil McCann and a Jörg Albertz penalty ensuring that the Ibrox men, for the first time in history, won the title at the ground of their greatest rivals. Celtic self-destructed, with the game in danger of being abandoned as their fans invaded the pitch to attack referee Hugh Dallas, who was struck on the head by several coins, the game being held up as he received treatment with blood pouring from a head wound. It was a day of shame for the host club and their fans . . . but Rangers were worthy champions.

Twenty-seven days later, to general apprehension, the two protagonists met again – this time at Hampden Park in the Scottish FA Cup Final, with Hugh Dallas again the referee. However, the game was a relatively tame affair decided in Rangers' favour by a Rod Wallace goal early in the second half. This had been the first big game to be staged at the newly renovated Mount Florida ground, but despite the millions spent at taxpayers' expense the stadium came up short compared to Ibrox.

On the European front Advocaat restored the club's pride with outstanding victories over PAOK Salonika (Arsenal's conquerors one year earlier) and Bundesliga giants Bayer Leverkusen. The UEFA Cup run ended in the last 16 at the hands of Parma, one of the giants of the European scene from Italy's Serie A. Rangers, however, would exact a full measure of revenge for their elimination by defeating the Italians eight months later in the Champions League qualifiers – a result that would arguably be Advocaat's finest hour as Ibrox boss.

There had been some severe disappointments in Europe in recent years, but such successes gave the Light Blue legions renewed hope that the days of glory against continental opposition were not all in the past.

Leading appearance maker: Sergio Porrini, 54 games
Leading goalscorer: Rod Wallace, 26 goals

— A SPAT WITH HEARTS —

In January 1899 Rangers played Hearts in a Scottish Cup tie at First Ibrox. The match was a feisty affair, and when Hearts' George Hogg was ordered off his teammates followed him off the field in protest at the decision. Play was held up for some time, before the Hearts players were persuaded to return to the pitch by their club officials. Rangers went on to win 4–1.

The following day, the players of both teams were heavily criticised in the sporting press, with *The Scottish Referee* describing the events at Ibrox as "The greatest blow to football since the institution of the Scottish FA in 1873." The report continued: "Many spectators have vowed not to return after witnessing such a spectacle. The display of feeling on the field and the low tactics of some of the players were worthy of the lowest class of rowdies that frequent our slums"

— RANGERS MANAGERS: ALEX MCLEISH (2001–06) —

Alex McLeish: two league titles

'Big Eck' arrived at the Stadium at a time of severe financial restrictions in December 2001, but at the same time inherited a squad of substantial quality from Dick Advocaat. He had previous managerial experience with both Motherwell and Hibernian, and won both League Cup and Scottish Cup during his first half-season in charge, defeating Martin O'Neill's Celtic *en route* to both.

The following campaign was a momentous one, with the club's seventh treble secured in the most nail-biting conclusion to a league season imaginable – Rangers winning the title by one goal from Celtic. Two years later the Light Blues again won the title on the final day when they defeated Hibernian 1–0 at Easter Road whilst Celtic, requiring three points to clinch the championship, lost 1–2 at Motherwell courtesy of two goals in the dying minutes of the game. This was perhaps McLeish's finest hour, as he ensured that momentum was maintained until the death even though Celtic led by five points with four games left to play. He left Ibrox in the summer of 2006, and after managing Scotland for a brief spell he returned to club football with Birmingham City.

Alex McLeish's honours:
League championship: 2002/03, 2004/05
Scottish Cup: 2002, 2003
Scottish League Cup: 2001/02, 2002/03, 2004/05

— THE BATTLE OF BARCELONA —

The final whistle in the 1972 European Cup Winners' Cup final in Barcelona was the cue for an exuberant pitch invasion by triumphant Rangers supporters. In an effort to clear the pitch of the celebrating fans the police, instead of ushering them off as Strathclyde's finest would undoubtedly have done, chose to attack viciously with batons flailing. The fans dispersed, regrouped on the far side of the ground, and to the absolute astonishment of the Spanish people, launched their own counter-attack.

As the battle raged on, the trophy was presented to John Greig deep inside the bowels of the Nou Camp. The Rangers fans had been denied the one sight they wanted to see above all others – their team with a European trophy.

It is of course true that the post-match incidents marred the achievement, but the damning publicity and condemnation heaped on Rangers by most of the Scottish press was harsh in the extreme and surely unjustified. A more balanced media view came from broadcaster Archie McPherson in his fascinating book *Action Replays* (Chapmans, 1991) who described the initial police baton charge as being like "a threshing machine". His account continued:

> *We thought it was over but to our astonishment we saw the supporters regrouping . . . they mounted a counter-attack. The police broke ranks and retreated . . . the supporters were giving as good as they got. "Any moment*

now the guns could come out, for God's sake" said Reuters'
correspondent in the area. I recall his words vividly. "What
you're seeing down there are Franco's men. They are not
Catalans. That is why they are so hated in this city."

Archie Macpherson's account will find sympathy and
understanding with all who were present in the Nou Camp –
but the Rangers support was unjustly condemned by the Scottish
press and by many sections of society who had not been present
in Barcelona. A statement from Glasgow's Labour Lord Provost
John Mains defied belief – he showed his true colours as he
described the behaviour of the fans as "shameful and
disgraceful". Yet when questioned about the brutality of the
Spanish police he replied, "I would not want to criticise because
I wasn't there."

The club's treatment at the hands of UEFA was scarcely any
better – a two-year ban reduced on appeal to one, although the
governing body did also ensure that Spain would not host another
European final for some ten years. Meanwhile for the local
citizens of Barcelona there was unreserved praise and admiration
for the Rangers fans who had achieved something no one had
dared even to contemplate before – they had fought back against
Franco's police.

— DYNAMIC ATTRACTION —

In 1945, in the slipstream of the Allied victory in the Second
World War, Dinamo Moscow visited Ibrox to play Rangers in a
friendly fixture. Ninety-five thousand spectators were witness to
a memorable 2–2 draw that is recalled with awe by those present
to this day, the fixture being the fourth and final game of a UK
tour by the Muscovites to cement sporting relations between two
nations that had fought the Axis Powers as partners in the global
conflict just concluded, but who would be on opposite sides of
the Iron Curtain in the Cold War that was about to envelop
Europe for the next 45 years.

— GREAT EUROPEAN NIGHTS AT IBROX 15 —

Rangers 1   Inter Milan 1
Løvenkrands Adriano

2005/06 UEFA Champions League Group H
6th December 2005
Attendance: 49,170

A tight Champions League group that saw Rangers up against Inter Milan, Porto and Artmedia Bratislava found the Glasgow club with matters in their own hands as they approached their sixth and final game.

It was all down to matchday six at Ibrox – all to play for, with Inter Milan due at Ibrox having already secured first place in the group. Nevertheless, the Italians opened the scoring in 28 minutes when an inswinging corner from Sinisa Mihajlovic found Adriano who was offered a free header. Ibrox was silenced – but only temporarily, for within eight minutes Rangers were level when a slide-rule pass from Thomas Buffel released Løvenkrands who coolly advanced on goalkeeper Francesco Toldo before slotting the ball home. The Italian giants were comfortable on the ball, their class, skill and vision all too apparent to knowing observers – but the home side gave as good as they got, and the scores were still level as the dying embers of the game approached.

Word had reached Glasgow that Artmedia and Porto remained goalless in Bratislava – a result that would send Rangers through. There being no further scoring at either venue, the Light Blues were through to the last 16 – and beleaguered manager Alex McLeish thus became the first Scottish club boss to guide his charges beyond the group stages of Europe's premier competition. He rightly regarded the achievement as one of the finest of his managerial career.

In the last 16 the Ibrox men were eliminated by Villarreal on away goals.

Rangers team: Waterreus; Ricksen, Murray; Kyrgiakos, Andrews, Ferguson; Burke, Malcolm, Lovenkrands, Buffel, Namouchi

— RANGERS' TRIPLE CROWNS: 2003 —

The most recent Triple Crown success for Rangers in season 2002/03 was the closest run campaign in Scottish football for almost 40 years.

Alex McLeish had succeeded Dick Advocaat in the manager's chair in December 2001 and had led the club to both League Cup and Scottish Cup in the next five months. He had inherited a strong squad from Advocaat, full of international talent of the ilk of Ronald de Boer, Shota Arveladze and Claudio Caniggia – and the following season would be a thrilling and nail-biting head-to-head with Martin O'Neill's Celtic, title winners for the previous two years.

Rangers made a strong start to the league race with eight wins from their first nine games – so that when they journeyed across the city on 6th October for the first Old Firm clash of the season they did so as championship leaders. A six-goal thriller ensued as a 3–3 draw retained the visitors' slender advantage – the most crucial goal being Rangers' second, a de Boer header from a Neil McCann cross, immediately after Celtic had gone into a 2–1 lead. Arguably the most important goal of the entire campaign. De Boer would prove to be the outstanding performer of the whole season, scoring a number of important goals, his blind-side runs constantly throwing opposition defences into chaos.

A 4–0 win at Tynecastle on 1st December underlined the class of the Ibrox men, and when Rangers hosted Celtic six days later it proved to be another high-scoring affair. The loss of a Chris Sutton goal after just 18 seconds (the fastest recorded goal in an Old Firm fixture) was overcome as Rangers swept into a 3–1 interval lead courtesy of goals from Craig Moore, de Boer (again) and Michael Mols. The final score of 3–2 underlined the Light Blue title credentials.

The first defeat of the domestic season was suffered at Motherwell on Boxing Day, with a controversial goal courtesy of 'old friend' referee Willie Young, but Rangers overcame that setback to win the next seven games before McLeish suffered his first reversal in an Old Firm fixture with a 0–1 loss at Parkhead on 8th March. There was no time to sulk however – one week later the first trophy of the season was secured in a 2–1 win over Celtic at Hampden in the League Cup Final, thanks to first-half goals from Claudio Caniggia and Peter Lovenkrands.

With five games left in the title race, Rangers led their great rivals by five points, but when Celtic won 2–1 at Ibrox in the fourth and final clash of the season it was all to play for. An astonishing game at Dundee ended 2–2 with the Ibrox men being awarded three penalties – two of which were missed by captain Barry Ferguson, to leave the two contenders level on points with three games to play.

So it remained on the final day of the season, which saw Rangers at home to Dunfermline Athletic and Celtic travel to Kilmarnock with Rangers holding the slenderest of leads on goals scored.

The destiny of the flag fluctuated throughout the afternoon as the goals flowed, but just when it appeared that Celtic had the upper hand a classic near-post de Boer header from a McCann cross gave Ibrox the advantage, never to be surrendered. Rangers triumphed 6–1 whilst Celtic won 4–0 at Rugby Park. The championship had been secured by one goal.

Six days later the Scottish FA Cup – and thus the treble – was secured with a 1–0 win over Dundee thanks to a Lorenzo Amoruso header midway through the second half. It was to be the Italian's final game in Light Blue.

On the European front, Rangers suffered their one major disappointment of the season when they were eliminated by Viktoria Zizkov of the Czech Republic on away goals.

Leading appearance maker: Stefan Klos, 50 games (ever-present)
Leading goalscorer: Ronald de Boer, 19 goals

— EUROPEAN FINALS: UEFA CUP, 2008 —

Rangers' run to the 2007/08 UEFA Cup Final was as unexpected as it was memorable. Following a third-place finish in their Champions League group, Rangers dropped into the last 32 of the UEFA Cup. A remarkable sequence of victories against Panathinaikos, Werder Bremen, Sporting Lisbon and Fiorentina saw the Ibrox men reach their fourth European final, 36 years after their triumph in Barcelona. The game was to be played in Manchester – against Russian champions Zenit Saint Petersburg, coached by former Rangers manager Dick Advocaat.

A Light Blue army estimated at perhaps 200,000 descended on Manchester, bringing the city centre almost to a complete standstill. The 'Gers support provided a colourful spectacle at a sun-bathed City of Manchester Stadium, with a capacity crowd comprising perhaps 75 per cent Rangers followers.

Rangers wore all blue, a kit favoured in European ties, although quite why this should be so is a bit of a mystery given that the first time such a strip was worn was in the Bernabeu in 1963 when the great Real Madrid team of that era overwhelmed a young 'Gers side 6–0.

Zenit started the more positive outfit, and threatened in three minutes when Steven Whittaker's error enabled Igor Denisov to release Andrei Arshavin who shot into the side-net, then eight minutes later Radek Sirl's 35-yard free kick was held by Neil Alexander, who was again called into action on 17 minutes when he held Konstantin Zyrianov's 25-yard shot.

It was all Zenit at this stage. Eleven minutes later Aleksandr Anyukov's swerving drive was held at the second attempt by the 'Gers goalkeeper. Rangers survived – and as the interval approached came more and more into the game. Indeed Kevin Thomson really should have done better than hit a 22-yard free kick straight into the wall.

The first half ended goalless. Rangers had two strong penalty claims turned down eight minutes after the restart following Zenit goalkeeper's Vyacheslav Malafeev's save from a Jean-Claude Darcheville shot from a Steve Davis pass, firstly for handball against a Russian defender, then as Barry Ferguson homed in on the loose ball he had his heels clearly clicked. The Scots were beginning to create chances – Whittaker saw a shot deflected wide in 63 minutes, then seconds later Davis' shot was cleared off the line by Anyukov.

In the next instant at the other end Arshavin was through on goal and after rounding the outrushing Alexander he saw his net-bound chip headed off the line by Saša Papac. It was now a much more open game and it was clear that the first goal was going to be crucial. Sadly it fell to Zenit – Igor Denisov coolly netting from a superb Arshavin pass.

Walter Smith recognised that he had to go for broke, introducing Nacho Novo, Lee McCulloch and Kris Boyd for Papac, Brahim Hemdani and Whittaker as Rangers ended up playing 4–3–3. Darcheville was almost through on a McCulloch headflick on 88 minutes only for a last-gasp intervention from Roman Shirokov. Sixty seconds later a long throw from Ferguson broke free in the box, but if anything too many Rangers players went for the ball, and Novo shot over the bar.

In the dying seconds Zenit clinched victory with a second goal when Man of the Match Arshavin released Fatih Tekke down the left, his cutback being turned into the net from point-blank range by Zyryanov.

Zenit were deserved victors, and as they were presented with the trophy they were applauded sportingly by both the Rangers players and fans. The dream was over. In truth, the Russian side were the better team – a class apart and the best by far that Rangers had played all season. They would form the core of the Russian side that would go on to reach the last four of Euro 2008.

UEFA Cup Final
Wednesday 14th May 2008
City of Manchester Stadium
Attendance: 47,000
Zenit Saint Petersburg 2 (Denisov, Zyryanov) Rangers 0
Rangers team: Alexander; Broadfoot, Weir, Cuellar, Papac (Novo); Davis, Hemdani (McCulloch), Ferguson, Thomson, Whittaker (Boyd); Darcheville

— BRAVEHEARTS —

Rangers players who were awarded medals in the Great War:

Player	Medal
Jock Buchanan	Distinguished Conduct Medal
Finlay Speedie	Military Medal
James Speirs	Military Medal
Dr James Paterson	Military Cross
Fred Gray	Military Cross
Walter Tull	British War and Victory Medal; Military Cross.

— PLAYER OF THE YEAR —

Rangers players to win the Scottish Football Writers' Association Footballer of the Year award are:

1966	John Greig
1972	Dave Smith
1975	Sandy Jardine
1976	John Greig
1978	Derek Johnstone
1989	Richard Gough
1992	Ally McCoist
1993	Andy Goram
1994	Mark Hateley
1995	Brian Laudrup
1996	Paul Gascoigne
1997	Brian Laudrup
2000	Barry Ferguson
2003	Barry Ferguson
2008	Carlos Cuellar

Andy Goram: 1993 Player of the Year

Rangers players to win the Scottish Professional Footballers' Association Players' Player of the Year award are:

1977/78	Derek Johnstone
1991/92	Ally McCoist
1992/93	Andy Goram
1993/94	Mark Hateley
1994/95	Brian Laudrup
1995/96	Paul Gascoigne
2001/02	Lorenzo Amoruso
2002/03	Barry Ferguson

— RANGERS MANAGERS: PAUL LE GUEN —

When Frenchman Paul Le Guen was appointed manager of Rangers in the summer of 2006 there was a great sense of anticipation and excitement amongst almost all friends of the club. This was a man with an impeccable track record, who as coach of Lyon had secured three successive titles in Le Championnat. However, his six months in Glasgow were less than successful, his signings in some instances disappointed and he returned to France in January 2007 to coach Paris Saint-Germain. By the time of his departure the league was effectively a lost cause and the League Cup lost, his one success being progress in the UEFA Cup with Auxerre, Livorno, Partizan Belgrade and Maccabi Haifa all overcome. His relative failure as Rangers manager was perhaps the greatest disappointment of chairman David Murray's time at the club.

— STALWART PERFORMERS —

Rangers' appearance records:

All games	Dougie Gray (1925–46) 945
Competitive fixtures	Dougie Gray (1925–46) 889
League games	Dougie Gray (1925–46) 667
	(includes 177 wartime)
	Sandy Archibald (1916–34) 514
European games	Barry Ferguson (1996–present) 82

— CLUB MOTTOS —

Rangers' original motto was *Aye Work Awa*, reflecting the work ethic of the youths, many of them young students, who founded the club in 1872.

A change to *Ready, Aye Ready* followed, subsequently shortened to *Aye Ready*. In 1966 a further abbreviated version was introduced in an attempt to embrace a more modern image – namely *Ready*, which endures to this day.

— SCOTTISH LEAGUE CUP TRIUMPHS —

Rangers have won the Scottish League Cup a record 25 occasions. Here are the details of the finals:

Season	Opponents	Venue	Attendance	Result
1946/47	Aberdeen	Hampden Park	83,684	4–0
1948/49	Raith Rovers	Hampden Park	57,450	2–0
1960/61	Kilmarnock	Hampden Park	82,063	2–0
1961/62	Hearts	Hampden Park	88,635	1–1
	Hearts (r)	Hampden Park	47,552	3–1
1963/64	Morton	Hampden Park	105,907	5–0
1964/65	Celtic	Hampden Park	91,423	2–1
1970/71	Celtic	Hampden Park	106,263	1–0
1975/76	Celtic	Hampden Park	58,806	1–0
1977/78	Celtic	Hampden Park	60,168	2–1
1978/79	Aberdeen	Hampden Park	60,000	2–1
1981/82	Dundee United	Hampden Park	53,777	2–1
1983/84	Celtic	Hampden Park	66,369	3–2
1984/85	Dundee United	Hampden Park	44,698	1–0
1986/87	Celtic	Hampden Park	74,219	2–1
1987/88	Aberdeen	Hampden Park	71,961	3–3*
1988/89	Aberdeen	Hampden Park	72,122	3–2
1990/91	Celtic	Hampden Park	62,817	2–1
1992/93	Aberdeen	Hampden Park	45,298	2–1
1993/94	Hibernian	Celtic Park	47,632	2–1
1996/97	Hearts	Celtic Park	48,559	4–3
1998/99	St Johnstone	Celtic Park	45,533	2–1
2001/02	Ayr United	Hampden Park	50,076	4–0
2002/03	Celtic	Hampden Park	52,000	2–1
2004/05	Motherwell	Hampden Park	50,182	5–1
2007/08	Dundee United	Hampden Park	50,019	2–2*

*Rangers won on penalties.

— MISCELLANEOUS SEASONAL RECORDS —

Highest points total: 97 (2002/03)
Most league wins: 35 (1920/21)
Fewest defeats: 0 (1898/99)
Lowest points total: 20 (1893/94)
Fewest league wins: 8 (1893/94)
Most defeats: 14 (1979/80 and 1985/86)
Most goals scored: 118 (1931/32 and 1933/34)
Fewest goals conceded: 15 (1897/98)
Fewest goals scored: 41 (1892/93 and 1894/95)
Most goals conceded: 55 (1925/26 and 1938/39)
Most draws: 14 (1993/94)
Fewest draws: 0 (1898/99)
Best goal difference: +81 (1919/20)
Worst goal difference: +4 (1979/80)
Most consecutive titles: 9 (1938/39–1946/47 and
1988/89–1996/97)
More than 100 goals scored in a season: 1919/20, 1927/28,
1928/29, 1931/32, 1932/33, 1933/34, 1935/36, 1938/39,
1991/92 and 2002/03

— CENTURIONS —

When Kris Boyd netted his 100th goal for Rangers on 25 April
2009 at Hampden Park in a 3–0 win over St. Mirren in the
Scottish FA Cup semi-final he joined an exclusive club. The
following players have likewise scored a century of goals in Light
Blue:

		Goals	Appearances
Jimmy Smith	1928–1946	382	411
Ally McCoist	1983–1998	355	581
Bob McPhail	1927–1940	287	465
Willie Thornton	1937–1954	248	410
Robert Hamilton	1897–1906 & 07-08	247	293
Jimmy Fleming	1925–1935	240	295
Willie Reid	1909–1920	226	262

Derek Johnstone	1970–1983 & 85-86	210	546
Ralph Brand	1954–1965	206	317
Alex Venters	1933–1946	205	407
Andy Cunningham	1915–1929	202	444
Alec Smith	1894–1915	201	654
John McPherson	1890–1902	173	324
Sandy Archibald	1917–1934	168	660
Billy Simpson	1950–1959	163	239
Jimmy Millar	1955–1967	162	317
Geordie Henderson	1919–1927	161	223
Tommy Cairns	1913–1927	159	497
Davie Wilson	1956–1967	157	373
Dr. James Marshall	1925–1934	153	260
Jimmy Duncanson	1939–1951	147	302
Jim Forrest	1960–1967	145	163
Willie Johnston	1964–1972 & 80-82	125	393
Max Murray	1955–1963	121	154
John Greig	1960–1978	120	755
Alan Morton	1920–1933	119	498
Mark Hateley	1990–1995 & 96-97	115	222
Derek Parlane	1970–1980	111	300
Alex Scott	1954–1963	108	331
Johnny Hubbard	1949–1959	106	238
Kris Boyd	2006–	102	153

— RANGERS LEAGUE RECORD 1890–2008 —

Season	Tier	P	W	D	L	F	A	Pts	Pos
1890/91	D1	18	13	3	2	58	25	29	1
1891/92	D1	22	11	2	9	59	46	24	5
1892/93	D1	18	12	4	2	41	27	28	2
1893/94	D1	18	8	4	6	44	30	20	4
1894/95	D1	18	10	2	6	41	26	22	3
1895/96	D1	18	11	4	3	57	39	26	2
1896/97	D1	18	11	3	4	64	30	25	3
1897/98	D1	18	13	3	2	71	15	29	2
1898/99	D1	18	18	0	0	79	18	36	1
1899/00	D1	18	15	2	1	69	27	32	1
1900/01	D1	20	17	1	2	60	25	35	1
1901/02	D1	18	13	2	3	43	29	28	1
1902/03	D1	22	12	5	5	56	30	29	3
1903/04	D1	26	16	6	4	80	33	38	4
1904/05	D1	26	19	3	4	83	28	41	2
1905/06	D1	30	15	7	8	58	48	37	4
1906/07	D1	34	19	7	8	69	33	45	3
1907/08	D1	34	21	8	5	74	40	50	3
1908/09	D1	34	19	7	8	91	38	45	4
1909/10	D1	34	20	6	8	70	35	46	3
1910/11	D1	34	23	6	5	90	34	52	1
1911/12	D1	34	24	3	7	86	34	51	1
1912/13	D1	34	24	5	5	76	41	53	1
1913/14	D1	38	27	5	6	79	31	59	2
1914/15	D1	38	23	4	11	74	47	50	3
1915/16	D1	38	25	6	7	87	39	56	2
1916/17	D1	38	24	5	9	68	32	53	3
1917/18	D1	34	25	6	3	66	24	56	1
1918/19	D1	34	26	5	3	86	16	57	2
1919/20	D1	42	31	9	2	106	25	71	1
1920/21	D1	42	35	6	1	91	24	76	1
1921/22	D1	42	28	10	4	83	26	66	2
1922/23	D1	38	23	9	6	67	29	55	1
1923/24	D1	38	25	9	4	72	22	59	1
1924/25	D1	38	25	10	3	76	26	60	1

1925/26	D1	38	19	6	13	79	55	44	6
1926/27	D1	38	23	10	5	85	41	56	1
1927/28	D1	38	26	8	4	109	36	60	1
1928/29	D1	38	30	7	1	107	32	67	1
1929/30	D1	38	28	4	6	94	32	60	1
1930/31	D1	38	27	6	5	96	29	60	1
1931/32	D1	38	28	5	5	118	42	61	2
1932/33	D1	38	26	10	2	113	43	62	1
1933/34	D1	38	30	6	2	118	41	66	1
1934/35	D1	38	25	5	8	96	46	55	1
1935/36	D1	38	27	7	4	110	43	61	2
1936/37	D1	38	26	9	3	88	32	61	1
1937/38	D1	38	18	13	7	75	49	49	3
1938/39	D1	38	25	9	4	112	55	59	1
1939/40	D1	30	22	4	4	72	36	48	1
1940/41	D1	30	21	4	5	79	33	46	1
1941/42	D1	30	22	4	4	97	35	48	1
1942/43	D1	30	22	6	2	89	23	50	1
1943/44	D1	30	23	4	3	90	27	50	1
1944/45	D1	30	23	3	4	88	27	49	1
1945/46	D1	30	22	4	4	85	41	48	1
1946/47	D1	30	21	4	5	76	26	46	1
1947/48	D1	30	21	4	5	64	28	46	2
1948/49	D1	30	20	6	4	63	32	46	1
1949/50	D1	30	22	6	2	58	26	50	1
1950/51	D1	30	17	4	9	64	37	38	2
1951/52	D1	30	16	9	5	61	31	41	2
1952/53	D1	30	18	7	5	80	39	43	1
1953/54	D1	30	13	8	9	56	35	34	4
1954/55	D1	30	19	3	8	67	33	41	3
1955/56	D1	34	22	8	4	85	27	52	1
1956/57	D1	34	26	3	5	96	48	55	1
1957/58	D1	34	22	5	7	89	49	49	2
1958/59	D1	34	21	8	5	92	51	50	1
1959/60	D1	34	17	8	9	72	38	42	3
1960/61	D1	34	23	5	6	88	46	51	1
1961/62	D1	34	22	7	5	84	31	51	2
1962/63	D1	34	25	7	2	94	28	57	1

1963/64	D1	34	25	5	4	85	31	55	1
1964/65	D1	34	18	8	8	78	35	44	5
1965/66	D1	34	25	5	4	91	29	55	2
1966/67	D1	34	24	7	3	92	31	55	2
1967/68	D1	34	28	5	1	93	34	61	2
1968/69	D1	34	21	7	6	81	32	49	2
1969/70	D1	34	19	7	8	67	40	45	2
1970/71	D1	34	16	9	9	58	34	41	4
1971/72	D1	34	21	2	11	71	38	44	3
1972/73	D1	34	26	4	4	74	30	56	2
1973/74	D1	34	21	6	7	67	34	48	3
1974/75	D1	34	25	6	3	86	33	56	1
1975/76	PD	36	23	8	5	60	24	54	1
1976/77	PD	36	18	10	8	62	37	46	2
1977/78	PD	36	24	7	5	76	39	55	1
1978/79	PD	36	18	9	9	52	35	45	2
1979/80	PD	36	15	7	14	50	46	37	5
1980/81	PD	36	16	12	8	60	32	44	3
1981/82	PD	36	16	11	9	57	45	43	3
1982/83	PD	36	13	12	11	52	41	38	4
1983/84	PD	36	15	12	9	53	41	42	4
1984/85	PD	36	13	12	11	47	38	38	4
1985/86	PD	36	13	9	14	53	45	35	5
1986/87	PD	44	31	7	6	85	23	69	1
1987/88	PD	44	26	8	10	85	34	60	3
1988/89	PD	36	26	4	6	62	26	56	1
1989/90	PD	36	20	11	5	48	19	51	1
1990/91	PD	36	24	7	5	62	23	55	1
1991/92	PD	44	33	6	5	101	31	72	1
1992/93	PD	44	33	7	4	97	35	73	1
1993/94	PD	44	22	14	8	74	41	58	1
1994/95	PD	36	20	9	7	60	35	69	1
1995/96	PD	36	27	6	3	85	25	87	1
1996/97	PD	36	25	5	6	85	33	80	1
1997/98	PD	36	21	9	6	76	38	72	2
1998/99	SPL	36	23	8	5	76	31	77	1
1999/00	SPL	36	28	6	2	96	26	90	1
2000/01	SPL	38	26	4	8	76	36	82	2

2001/02	SPL	38	25	10	3	82	27	85	2
2002/03	SPL	38	31	4	3	101	28	97	1
2003/04	SPL	38	25	6	7	76	33	81	2
2004/05	SPL	38	29	6	3	78	22	93	1
2005/06	SPL	38	21	10	7	67	37	73	3
2006/07	SPL	38	21	9	8	61	32	72	2
2007/08	SPL	38	27	5	6	84	33	86	2

— 'SCOTTISH PREMIER LEAGUE ALL-TIME TABLE' —

P	Club	Ssn	Pld	W	D	L	F	A	GD	Pts
1	Celtic	11	414	304	61	49	968	336	+632	973
2	Rangers	11	414	282	76	56	876	333	+543	922
3	Hearts	11	414	172	103	39	560	487	+73	619
4	Aberdeen	11	414	147	98	169	499	587	-88	539
5	Kilmarnock	11	414	146	100	168	507	591	-84	538
6	Hibernian	10	378	137	97	144	526	526	0	508
7	Motherwell	11	414	133	94	187	500	630	-130	493
8	Dundee United	11	414	112	115	187	451	636	-185	451
9	Dunfermline	8	302	78	79	145	295	483	-188	313
10	Dundee	7	262	80	61	121	308	412	-104	301
11	Inverness CT	5	190	60	48	82	222	253	-31	228
12	Livingston	5	190	48	45	97	205	306	-101	189
13	Falkirk	4	152	45	35	72	166	212	-46	170
14	St Johnstone	4	148	39	43	66	139	200	-61	160
15	St Mirren	4	152	35	39	78	122	229	-107	144
16	Partick Thistle	2	76	14	19	43	76	125	-49	61
17	Hamilton Accies	1	38	12	5	21	30	53	-23	41
18	Gretna	1	38	5	8	25	32	83	-51	13*

* Gretna were deducted 10 points for going into administration in the 2007/08 season

ROBERT MCELROY

Robert McElroy is the editor of *The Rangers Historian* magazine, first published in 1987. He is also the author of the following titles which may be of interest to readers of *The Rangers Miscellany*:

Rangers Player by Player (1990, Crowwood Press and updated 1997 & 1998, Hamlyn)

Rangers Season by Season (1992, True Blue Publications)

The Rangers Annual 1992 (Holmes McDougall)

Rangers: The Complete Record (1996 and updated 2005, Breedon Books)

Images of Scotland – Rangers Football Club 1872–1964 (1998 and updated 2003, Tempus Publishing)

The Spirit of Ibrox (1999, Lancaster Publishing)

Football Memorabilia (1999, Carlton Books)

The Enduring Dream (2006, Tempus Publishing)